The Smoking and Curing Book

By
Paul Peacock

Published 2007
Reprinted 2009

ISBN 978-1-904871-61-3

A catalogue record for this book is available from
the British Library.

Published by
The Good Life Press Ltd.,
PO Box 536
Preston
PR2 9ZY
www.goodlifepress.co.uk
www.homefarmer.co.uk

Cover design and drawings by Firecatcher Books.

Printed in Great Britain
By Cromwell Press Group

Contents

Preface

This book is written by way of a confession. I have to admit to an unhealthy fascination, no - an obsession, with fried eggs. When I first started to keep my own hens I was completely mesmerised by the joy of taking a fresh egg, preferably from beneath a still clucking hen, and rushing it to the kitchen to fry.

The white would not rush about the pan as though it were the spring tide. It would hold its shape, the perfect backdrop for the yolk, golden, pert, promising and standing proud and outdoing the sun in its glory. Time and again I was grateful to my hens for providing food that was fit for a king, especially compared to the eggs I bought from the supermarket whose shells often belied the travesty within.

Fresh eggs, really fresh eggs, ruined my breakfast. The bacon swam around the pan, not fried but more poached in its own excess liquids, smeared with fat that emulsified rather than rendered into the pan and sliced so thin that whatever flavour remained in the cooked meat was not recognised by my tongue.

My plate became schizophrenic. The glory of eggs revealed the shame of what I had become used to as bacon. The only thing I could do was to buy ever more expensive bacon, which I could not really afford so dried cured bacon came to make the English national dish enjoyable only as a rarity. Not a good state of affairs for a "Full English" Englishman.

How difficult could it be to make your own bacon? After all I had built a hencoop, found a supply of grain, bought birds, clipped their wings and treated them for red mite and had even found out how near they were to laying by playing with their bottoms! If I could do all this to provide the kings and queens of eggs for my family, why should I not cure my own bacon?

And why not indeed!

The process started for me in an old plastic dish. I simply bought some belly pork and covered it with a mixture of salt and sugar. The following morning the dish was filled with liquid and I washed the meat, which now looked like children who had been swimming all day at the local municipal baths.

I washed it and sliced it with my sharpest knife, which was nothing like sharp enough, and dried it on a towel. In the pan the meat changed colour and looked a bit grey, as though I had fried my own fingers. The flavour, however, was a complete revelation. For the first time I cooked a bacon and egg sandwich which oozed both yolk and pride. Both dribbled down my chin, the yolk onto my shirt, and the pride onto my smile. They say the very best seasoning is pride, and I cannot deny that I had found the perfect match to my eggs; my breakfast plate was well again.

In this book you will find many techniques and recipes. Everything has been tested, proof of which can be found in my ample girth, which is now decreasing because of an increase in activity rather than a reduced intake. Well, even a "Full English" Englishman has his limits.

Happy curing!

Paul Peacock

Manchester 2007.

Introduction

This is an important part of the book so please do not skip it!

I would like to put my cards on the table. In some respects there is a big tension in my mind about this book because in reality I abhor people messing about with food. I don't like E-numbers, preservatives, additives, colourings, stabilisers and anything else that means some fat cat industrialist can get his product on the shelf for long enough for me to buy it. It is a form of slavery when all you can buy is their food, and no amount of them saying that it's a good product, wholesome and fit for purpose, will change my mind.

But here I am advocating the use of a couple of additives; E249 to E252 respectively, and common salt. Somehow it goes against the grain but this is offset by saying that the saltpetre and associated nitrites have been used for centuries to preserve food, and as we shall read later, they mimic one of the important natural processes our bodies use when it comes to fighting bacteria.

The other 'beef' I have, if you will pardon the pun, is against machine made food. A pork pie made by hand is such a different food to one churned out by some machine. The only way I can explain it is that the machine lacks something; perhaps the human touch.

Perhaps it is that very human touch which means that we end up doing an awful lot of things with our hands that have no place in the kitchen and consequently it is important to remember that the first rule of curing, in common with all food handling, is a complete fastidiousness about cleanliness.

Some rules

You will possibly get bored with this book repeating the mantra of cleanliness all the time and on every page. You might even get to the point where you are tempted to throw the book across the kitchen but don't ever say I didn't warn you of the following:

- Sprinkling salt on a worktop does not sterilise it! Use Milton or bleach or an anti-bacterial spray.

- Wearing plastic gloves doesn't mean they're clean! Change them as often as you would wash your hands.

- Flashing boiling water around does not clean things! Use a detergent and an abrasive cleaner.

- Knives need cleaning too.

- Chopping boards can have more bacteria on them than toilets.

- Refrigerators can actually be really slow incubators. Smoking alone does not make food safe.

- Store your utensils dry, but let them air dry rather than wiping them with a soiled tea towel.

- Keep your hair out of the way, don't bite your nails and use a handkerchief, preferably in another room.

- Wear a clean apron.

How to use this book

It's scary writing a book like this. One wants people to read and enjoy it but also to learn from it and hopefully not to poison themselves in the process of tasting its fruits. Please do not attempt to cure meat and fish with one eye on the food and another in this book. Instead, try to get the whole picture by reading it in its entirety and then experiment by sticking to the rules. (Yes, I know that doesn't make sense, but you know what I mean.)

Do not scrimp on cleanliness and do not skimp on food safety. Beyond this, get a pencil out and start to scribble; make notes, try the recipes, taste them, amend them, even reject them if you must.

If the end product tastes too salty you can always wash it to remove the salt but beware! Do not try to cure food without using salt.

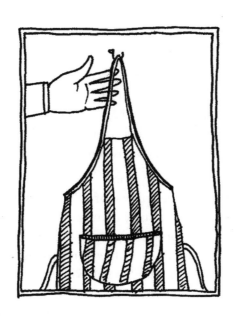

Chapter One
Ripping Yarns And Other Meats

Wherever we go these days there is a huge amount of ready prepared food. We seem to believe that it should be available more or less on tap. We do not, however, seem willing to put any kind of effort into making this food. For example, if we want bacon we go and buy it or we click on a computer screen and a bunch of electrons instructs a human being somewhere else to deliver it to our door. We do not give any thought to how the bacon came to our door, what chemicals went into it, or even if we are getting value for our money. Indeed, banks and shops do not want us to see money at all, just credit and we take it for granted that good quality safe food can be bought from a shop which offers us that credit.

Because of this we have become separated from the processes that make food. We have bacon because we like bacon, not because we have spare pig meat and need to stop it from going bad. Today cured, smoked, pickled and salted meat, fish and cheese are consumed because of their flavour and not out of necessity.

The growth in convenience has been largely at the expense of knowledge and skill. But if you are reading this, and have perhaps bought the book, (in which case thank you!) you are likely to be one of those people who, like me, feel strongly that the skills involved in making, and indeed growing our own food, should be relearned.

Why? Well firstly to be totally sure of what chemicals are in our food and to be in complete control of what we put on our family's dinner plates. Secondly, there may come a time when these life skills might become more important to people. We can not always be sure how our food will come to us in these uncertain times. The Bible even tells us that we should not "perish for lack of knowledge." We now compete in a global market for food that was once made on our doorstep but you cannot be sure that we will be able to continue to compete in the same way in the future. Many foods may fall by the wayside because not enough people choose to buy them. Try to buy tripe! It's not as easy as you might think but would you know how to make it?

For the time being at least, the most important reason for learning the theory and practise of smoking and curing is that it adds pride to our cooking, and pride is a seasoning of greater worth than the very best salt. Maybe, just maybe, one day your skills will be handed down to a grateful grandchild who for the first time may have to preserve or make food out of necessity.

Fish

The UK has the best seafood in the world bar none. The waters around the UK have the right mix of cold and warm waters, mixed with just the right minerals to have created the conditions for the very best seafood from shellfish to cod and salmon.

Anyone who has caught fish in the sea, particularly mackerel, will know that they are completely different in texture when you finally get them home. Imagine a slow journey by horse or on foot that takes several days and the effect this time will have on the condition of the fish. Fresh sea food has always been a feature of most coastal towns but traditionally the rest of us had to make do with fresh water or salted fish. Quick transport and a cheap freezing process now make the taste of fresh sea fish commonplace, but there are still plenty of smoked and salted products which make up many of our staple foods.

When you consider the quality of our produce, the salted and smoked varieties are clearly also some of the best in the world, but we consider them to be somehow inferior, as though their commonplace nature has left them undesirable. If kippers were French, Chinese or Japanese they would probably have people singing their praises and declaring their worth at every opportunity. We perhaps need to celebrate our own British cuisine.

As an example, many people have taken to cooking lobster for themselves. They nip out to the supermarket and buy a lobster that was dragged from the sea in Canadian waters, then shipped across the Atlantic, processed in Hull and driven to supermarkets all over the country.

The poor shopper doesn't realise that the British lobster is so much superior to its American counterpart. It tastes better and is bigger but we never buy them; they virtually all go to Spain and France where people congratulate themselves on knowing about food!

Meat

As an animal dies its death does not necessarily mean anything to its muscles for several minutes other than that the signals from the nervous system react violently due to changes in the concentration of salts in the tissue. The animal's muscles, now joints of meat, are still alive and active, and can contract, which they invariably do. The remaining ATP molecules are used up and consequently, within a few hours, all the muscles become stiff. This is called rigor mortis. As all the oxygen in the body is used the cells switch into anaerobic mode, and this form of respiration releases lactic acid. The increasing acidity starts to break down the muscles, and this process reduces the stiffening. The muscles are now beginning to break up and become tender.

This is critical to the process of hanging meat. What is really going on is the deterioration of the muscle tissue and a subsequent increase in bacterial action. It should not be allowed to continue indefinitely. Seemingly macho statements like 'let it hang for a month' or 'it should be almost rotten before you eat it' should be taken, quite literally, with a large pinch of salt. If you are preserving your own food you should start with the freshest possible ingredients before any bacteria have had a chance to grow to appreciable numbers.

Bacteria increase the process of decomposition, partly because they are releasing more acid into the meat and partly because they are actually living in the meat, using it as food. Eventually the waste products from the bacteria increase until the meat is spoiled and dangerously inedible. Flesh then turns black and begins to smell, sometimes oozing liquids.

It is the blood in the meat that first starts the rotting process; it is rich in nutrients and an excellent food for pathogenic organisms. Sometimes you see blackish or very dark meat in the shops. This is partly due to the breakdown of blood.

Mass murder

Bacteria grow exponentially in all kinds of untreated meat. You must be careful to stick to the rules regarding hanging, keeping and curing. If the bacterial population is doubling every twenty minutes, food that is fit to eat one day will be dangerous the next. Be completely sure about the freshness of your produce and utterly fastidious about cleanliness and your control of what is going on and if you are going to feed your creations to anyone other than your self, be totally sure you can do so with complete safety.

I have an extreme aversion to being remembered as a mass murderer. The word botulism came into the language because of a single example of poisoning by sausages in Germany. Under no circumstances should you look to secure your place in history by repeating this dubious achievement.

The increase in the bacterial population of the meat can be halted in three ways; by cooking, freezing or preserving. One important consideration is that poisoning does not only occur from the presence of live unwanted bacteria in our gut, but also from the waste products of bacteria, alive or otherwise.

It can be argued that smoking was the original method of curing. Food left hanging around a hearth or a fire would have become smoked and consequently would have lasted longer. The history of curing is, however, largely the history of salt.

The use of salt by mankind predates the development of agriculture and is estimated to be at least 25,000 years old but its use in preserving was probably associated with the widespread introduction of agriculture some 10,000 years ago. One of the first animals to be domesticated for food was the sheep and consequently, in order to save as much meat as possible each year, salted lamb must surely have become the first preserved delicacy known to man.

There are recipes for salted lamb that reach far back into antiquity, many still enjoyed in large quantities in Scandinavia. Pinnekjøtt from Norway is a dish of salted lamb ribs, Saltkjöt is salted mutton eaten with pea soup. Salted lamb is, however, now largely restricted to these countries

How salt preserves

Food is spoiled by insects, fungi and bacteria. On the face of it there is nothing wrong with eating meat with maggots in it. Indeed, this was the basis of the average British sailor's menu for many hundreds of years. It was not very appetising, but was generally safe. However, given certain circumstances, fungi and bacteria can do us a great deal of harm, and it is these unseen organisms which present the greatest risk to our health when eating.

Everyone needs salt in order to survive. Our bodies use salt for all kinds of functions; metabolic chemistry in the liver and blood, nervous chemistry in the axioms, your spinal cord and renal chemistry in the kidneys. But when there is too much salt in the body, problems begin to occur. These problems help us to understand precisely what happens when salt is used as a preservative.

Too great a concentration of salt in the blood will pull water from your tissues and you will become thirsty as a result. Your blood pressure will increase and you could become dangerously ill. In a piece of dead meat, the addition of salt does exactly the same thing; it pulls water from the tissues. This process is violently powerful. If the concentration is high enough the water will be pulled from the cells so quickly that the cell wall will rupture.

On this planet we are aware that life cannot exist without water. If you remove the water from microscopic life forms such as bacteria and fungi then these organisms will die and the food will remain unspoiled.

The same thing happens when sugar is used as a preservative. The major problem with sugar is simply that it is not as effective as salt at doing the same job. Scientists talk of the osmotic gradient, the difference between the concentration of salt and pure water on either side of the microbe's cell wall. With salt this osmotic gradient is much higher than with sugar and consequently the water is forced out of the microbe more violently.

Many cure recipes call for salt and sugar. The sugar is often only there for taste, frequently in commercial products where it can serve to disguise the flavour of the salt.

Most of the methods of preserving food act by removing water or making it impossible for microbes to use the water in the food. But there are others.

Poison

A lot of curing is done by adding a substance to food that is actually toxic to microbes, and since we dedicate a whole chapter to nitrates and nitrites, we will not mention them in any further detail here.

Cooking

Cooking is possibly the oldest way of preserving food. It is short in action and depends on killing all the microbes. This involves heating until it attains a temperature of 75°C for around 15 minutes. This does not ensure that the food is completely sterile, although it does come close. It takes around three days to a week for cooked food to go off, depending on the conditions in which it is kept.

If you cook your food there are a number of ways to keep the bacteria out of it and consequently to increase the chances of it lasting longer. A confit is an ancient form of preservation. Indeed, the word means to preserve.

Making a confit

The idea is to cook your meat in fat. The meat needs to be cooked until it is falling off the bone. This is important because the salmonella bug grows in the membrane between the muscle and the bone.

You can remove the bones, and the meat can then be pressed together and returned to the fat, which is allowed to cool naturally. You now have a dish of fat with some meat inside. Bacteria do not grow very well in fat and so the confit will last for up to a month. The excess fat can be removed before serving. It is also a good way of cooking whole legs. The confit is usually used for poultry, but similar principles are used in preserving pork.

Making a ham (see chapter 4) has a stage where the cure and spices have been added and cleaned away and the meat is hung, having been covered in lard to keep microbes away.

Duck or Goose fat are probably the best to use for this process because they readily render in manageable quantities. Pork fat will also do the job but in order to make the fat you have to roast a larger piece of meat or render a lot of fat.

The traditional confit does not have any salt except for flavouring, but it is not a huge leap of the imagination to realize that salted confits will last longer than unsalted ones. It is probably as a result of these realizations that the preserving qualities of salt first became known and it is almost certainly the improvements in the technology of cooking which led to the growth of agriculture.

Pies

The combination of wheat flour and fat to create an airtight paste into which is cooked meat or fish or almost anything is another way of prolonging the preserving effect of food. This was one of the original uses of pastry. The problem with pastry, however, is that it does absorb water and juices from the cooking, and so becomes an excellent medium for microbial growth. A sealed uncut pie will last for a week and will last for two weeks if it is completely filled with salty jelly. Actually, in our house they usually only last a couple of hours.

Drying

The basic idea behind drying food is the same as most processes of preservation; the removal of water. Since the invention of fire, food has always been dried, but the method is not that easy to be sure of. Thick pieces of meat might well be dried for preservation on the outside, but some way inside, the temperature and conditions might just be perfect for bacterial growth.

It is for precisely this reason that a combination of processes have evolved. Drying only thin sheets of material will ensure that the food is uniformly dehydrated and is a very common process. Drying associated with salting is also common, particularly for wet, sweet material such as pork and fish.

These processes significantly change the food from the fresh original. Changes in consistency and flavour create an entirely different product, and this is further enhanced by the addition of spices and herbs to foods. Dried beef is no longer beef; dried pork becomes ham and so on.

The simplest drying methods are by fires, and no doubt this led directly to smoking as a methodology. These days we can dry in our kitchens, as they have done in farmhouses for centuries, or in special drying chambers. You can buy desiccators that force the water out of food, or you can maintain a humidity controlled environment in almost any cabinet.

It should be pointed out that all foods can be dried; seeds, beans, peas, corn, fruit, tomatoes etc. Indeed, almost anything. A simple dryer made from plastic can be used in the summertime. It has clear plastic on the sunny side, black plastic on the other and a good plastic floor. The energy from the sun causes evaporation and the food dries out fairly easily. You simply cannot beat homemade sun dried tomatoes!

Jerky

When people buy those little plastic bags of hard meat from the supermarket they probably don't realise that they are eating one of the oldest preserved foods known to man. Jerky is thin strips of beef dried and sometimes smoked. It is usually, though not always, salted. The basic principle behind this type of preservation is the removal of water to such an extent that microbes can no longer reproduce in the meat. The bacteria are not necessarily dead, just dormant.

This illustrates an important principle. Humans can easily cope with some poisonous bacteria; it is when they are ingested in reasonably large numbers that problems occur, though the actual number of pathogenic bacteria it takes to make you ill does vary. A single piece of infected meat can be enough.

Meat is difficult to dry. It is thick and spongy and can absorb water from the atmosphere quite easily. Meat is so hungry for water that some unscrupulous manufacturers actually sold machines to add water to meat with the advertising tag: "Why sell meat when you can sell water?" Even today supermarkets still get away with selling meat with added water, describing it as good for the consistency of the product.

Thinly sliced meat is much easier to dry sufficiently to make its preservation safe. There is plenty of deterioration of the product, both nutritionally and in taste. This kind of food helped to facilitate the migration of peoples but its success was dependent on good cutting technology to make the slices and a decent fire to dry them out. Coated in fat, lightly smoked and wrapped in skins, jerky would last for up to six months.

Dried fish

You can buy a lot of dried fish these days which can easily be reconstituted with water. Usually salted and then left to hang, this product is easy to dry because, on the whole, fish are thin and some of them come ready salted!

Mackerel are the best to salt down when first caught. They are to be killed straight away then gutted, washed and laid in a bucket with salt sprinkled over them. I like to put a wooden board over them with a large rock on top to squash them flat.

While you are at it you can cook yourself a few on the beach; there is nothing better, but you would need a secluded beach indeed to build yourself a fire as such things seem to be frowned on these days although with good reason, I suppose, because too many people would not be prepared to clean up after themselves.

Salted fish are easy to dry at home and can be hung in an old fridge or a smoking chamber. However, buying fish from a shop to dry and smoke is not always a good idea. The fresher the fish, the better the result will be and the fish you buy from shops is often just too old.

When buying fish for smoking look for eyes that are completely clear, so that you could almost imagine that it is still alive, and a gloss on the skin that looks wet and shiny. Lost scales and scabby skins are a sign that the fish has been mishandled and it goes without saying that these fish should not be used.

Other produce such as cockles, mussels, whelks and limpets are also frequently cured or pickled in brine, mostly for travelling and shelving. If you are lucky enough to live by the sea I suppose you could collect food at any time. The rest of us have to do it in batches and later in the book you will find recipes for potted shrimp, cockles and many other types of produce without a backbone.

Freezing

This does not preserve meat; it simply holds it in time. Bacteria reproduce at room temperature at a rate that means they double in number every 20 minutes. In the freezer they reproduce at a rate that means they would double only every hundred years, but they are still alive in a dormant condition.

When the food thaws the bacteria go mad, reproducing very quickly because it seems to them to be their only chance. Their thawed life is made easier by the fact that the freezing process wrecks the natural structure of many foods, spilling nutrients into the meat itself. On the whole frozen meat should not be cured for keeping after thawing. By all means make a product such as bacon that will be eaten within a few days, but do not try to make a ham.

Vinegar

There is a huge difference between pickling vegetables and pickling meat and fish. The basic preservative is still salt when fish and meats are pickled. Herring, for example, are salted first and then cooked in pickle or brine. The vinegar is the means by which the food, now preserved in salt and sterile after having been boiled or heated, is kept germ free. Do not just throw some gutted herring in vinegar or you will end up with nothing more than a mess.

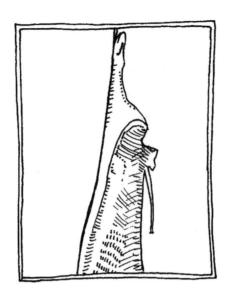

Chapter Two
A Word About Fresh Ingredients

The average shopper in the UK does not have an adequate understanding of what constitutes good produce. Freshness is measured in relation to the 'sell by' date printed on the packet rather than the fitness of the produce for a particular dish or cured product.

Of course the 'sell by' date is important if only for one simple reason; it protects the supermarket from selling food that might be off. But you can still buy a piece of meat or fish that is completely wrong for your intended purpose even though the 'sell by' and packaging might say otherwise.

Recognising good pork

If you get the feeding regime of pigs wrong and they are over fed or fed too much roughage or protein, this will be reflected in the quality and texture of the meat. Overfed pigs lay down a lot of fat and pigs denied the chance of walking around or digging and living a 'normal' life can produce a meat which is more gelatinous. The demarcation between fat and muscle can become indistinct which can make it difficult to remove the fat if the need arises.

The meat should not be granular in any way but should have a uniform pinkish colour with slight undulations in the texture, almost as though the muscle reveals itself in waves. This esoteric description covers the multitude of nuances that indicate good meat. If it is shiny, has plumpness and is moist, with flesh coloured skin that does not fall away from the meat then you can be sure it is good and fresh.

As meat ages the skin dries at a different rate from the muscle. This means that the joint will eventually begin to fall apart. The muscle will lose colour and become blotchy. If the meat has been soaked to increase its weight, or has been injected, the cut surface may well ooze slightly.

Recognising good meat

Beef, regardless of the cut, should have a distinct marbling of fat, only really visible if the meat is fresh. The muscle should appear filled with blood and shiny. If it looses its hue and begins to look brown, purple or grey, it is an older cut. Fat should be almost white, and since it yellows with age this is a good way of telling good beef.

The muscle is naturally grainier than pork and slightly ridged. The 'grain' has a definite direction and the meat should smell almost metallic. Once butchered, beef is then matured for varying lengths of time. This hanging very much reflects modern tastes, as though every slice of meat was of restaurant quality and consumed almost immediately after purchase.

Beef that is to be cured should be as fresh as possible. The tastes of modern gastronomes who like rare steaks cut with blunt knives, should not be catered for if you are going to preserve your beef for any length of time. You need as few microbes in the meat as possible.

Lamb is an altogether more difficult meat to cure because of its fat content. Fat disrupts the flow of water and thus the distribution of ions of sodium and nitrate/nitrite. As referred to earlier salted lamb dishes are still available in Scandinavia, but are not really eaten elsewhere. When people needed a lamb to eat they killed it and cooked it fresh. Consequently there is a history of eating mutton, which is simply a lamb older than one year.

Good lamb is invariably fresh. It is darker in colour than pork and somewhat bruised looking all over, but certainly not purple or very dark brown. A good piece of lamb is mildly reminiscent of chocolate, and the fat is thin and slightly creamy in colour.

Smoked turkey and smoked chicken aside, there is not much need for preserved poultry for much the same reasons as sheep. However, if you haven't eaten salted sandwich chicken it could be said that you haven't lived and hot smoked chicken and turkey are lovely.

Chickens and turkeys should have clean flesh with no bruising. The skin should be pale and if you get the chance to pinch it, the skin should bounce back to its position firmly and quickly. Turkeys are frozen for most of the year save Christmas, so do not try to preserve this meat in any way, except perhaps as an ingredient in sausage that will be eaten quickly and not frozen. Corn fed chickens are yellowish, but uniformly so. Sometimes you see birds that have a yellow staining, but are not corn fed. Avoid them!

Pheasants are frequently hung, and consequently are of little use for preserving. We do have a recipe for confit. If this is to be made using pheasant that is freshly killed it is sure to last the week out.

Offal

Livers, kidneys, hearts, brains, stomachs and lungs are all fine foods to be made the most of, even if you only use them as a basis for stock. Offal is best used as fresh as possible and is not really used in preserved products, save perhaps in patés, which should not be kept for more than a few days anyway. The nose is the best guide to the freshness of offal.(See The Sausage Book for Black Pudding recipes.)

Tripe is not cured, only cleaned and par-boiled before cooking again at home. It goes off quickly and should be consumed straight away.

Recognising good fish

A fresh fish should look as though it might swim away if you gave it a good poke. The eyes should be clear, almost clear enough to wink at you, without any creaminess. The skin should be fully scaled, slime free and not patchy. Although it might smell fishy, it should have no taint. The gills should be pink, not grey.

Molluscs

All molluscs should be alive before you cook and preserve them. To confirm this, tap them on the bench and see if they close. Any that do not respond are dead and should be discarded. Be sure they are fit to eat. Even a live cockle or mussel might be unfit for consumption if they were living in a soiled part of a beach.

If a mollusc shows only a sluggish response, discard it.

Lobsters and crabs

These animals should be alive when you start to cook them. There are no perfect ways of killing them. Plunging a knife into them will not kill, it simply gets on their nerves. Putting them into boiling water from fresh kills them in a few seconds but it is unpleasant watching them try to get out of the pan during this time which can seem like an eternity to the helpless bystander.

The best way to kill them is to put them in the fridge, then the freezer, where they go into a catatonic state, oblivious to the world. A few hours in the freezer should be sufficient. Then plunge them into a pan of boiling water. There will be no complaints and they will feel no pain.

Prawns and shrimps

The only way of telling if they are fresh is to confirm that they are still wriggling about when you drop them into the boiling pan, on or near the beach. Once cooked they turn pink and rise at which point they should be netted off and peeled before making wonderful potted confits!

What goes in my belly

I have a pet notion that the very best food, regardless of which restaurants you go to or which celebrity chef you might know, should be cooked and eaten at home. Two hundred years ago all the dishes that appear in this book were being cooked by ordinary people in ordinary homes but probably out of necessity, and with all our technology, our supermarkets and our television cookery programmes (and cookery books for that matter), how much better do you think they are today in the shops? The very best food you eat will probably be made by yourself, and when you allow a business to have sole control of what goes into your belly you may well find yourself worse off. When profit motivates the cook, the quality of the food can occasionally be the price you pay.

That said, there are still dedicated craftsmen making food and selling their wares but by making your own food such as bacon, ham, sausages etc., you at least have the opportunity to put exactly what you like in that food. This is a fundamental lesson every shopper could benefit from; just because you can buy cock-a-leekie soup in a tin does not mean that cock-a-leekie soup actually should be like that and just because bacon is salty in the shops does not mean that it has to be salty when you make it yourself.

Neither does a product have to contain numerous chemicals just to make it last longer on the shelf, or to stop it losing its colour.

E-numbers

As we have already pointed out, curing and smoking adds some E-numbers to your food. My argument about most of these chemicals is that they are not necessary to make the food. Some are fairly innocuous substances like guar gum or sediment agents which prevent tinned soup from forming into a mud at the bottom of the tin if left to stand for long periods. Others, however, have quite rightly earned a more ominous reputation.

Another problem is that we don't know the difficulties associated with these substances, even if we look them up. Science is continuously finding problems and something we felt was safe at one time may become the next revolting additive to send us into an early grave.

When curing there should be no need to put any substances in our food except for salt, saltpetre if called for and perhaps sugar. This applies even if you are selling your products as a small producer.

E100 - E199. These are largely colour enhancers and dyes. The basic concept is that if meat looks pink on the shelf, people will buy it. But meat is not naturally pink! Colour is often seen as the biggest problem by producers. Natural dyes and pigments are coloured because light excites electrons in a set of complex molecules but if they are being excited they can easily shoot off altogether and the substance will then lose its colour. A stabiliser will replace electrons knocked off the pigments, or will stop them shooting off in the first place. E101 (vitamin B2) is a naturally occurring stabiliser but E127 is erythosine, a molecule with well documented health implications.

What is wrong with selling 'meat' coloured meat. It was the normal practice when butchers were commonplace on the high street.

E200 - E299. These are preservatives. The problem with salt is that it is corrosive, and this has to be addressed by using certain types of container. These preservatives are not there to cure the meat, but to make it look edible. They do not stop it from rotting but keep the product looking fresh to prolong the shelf life. Some of these chemicals occur naturally in the body, such as E201, sodium sorbate. Others are not so nice. E218 (methyl parahydroxybenzoate), has been implicated in hormone based cancers.

E300 - E399. This group of chemicals are antioxidants and acidity buffers. E300 is in fact vitamin C. They are needed to keep the chemistry stable. Changes in acidity can drastically affect the food, changing the colour, flavour and texture.

E400 - E599. These are mineral components of food, sometimes caking agents or anti-caking agents, stabilisers, emulsifiers and thickeners such as guar gum. They tend to be harmless and inert.

E600 - E699. This is the group that includes monosodium glutamate or E624. It makes me feel ill but is said to be safe if you listen to the proprietor of my local Chinese take away. They are a group of flavour enhancers which inevitably prompts me to ask why I might wish to taste MSG when I could be enjoying the taste of the food as it is supposed to taste.

Spice is nice

Cured food does not contain much in the way of spice. On the whole spice is a disguise, not of poor quality meat, as some would suppose, but of vegetables. If everything tastes of a certain food or has a certain range of flavours then you can create a perfectly good vegetarian dish without missing the absence of meat.

Spices do not cure, they flavour. In spicing a cured product such as spicy bacon ribs, the spicing element is actually separate to the curing. Where you are combining the two processes do not dilute the amount of cure thinking the spice will do the job in its place.

Of course spices are an important part of pickles, but the basic cure is more important and comes well before flavour in the list of safety considerations.

The same goes for honey. Some have been caught out thinking that if they smear or soak their meat in honey it will be cured in the process. Honeyed food, such as a glazed ham or spiced honey bacon, must also be completely cured.

The golden rule when making highly spiced products is to get the cure right and then to get the flavour right.

Chapter Three
It'll Be All Right On The Nitrite

L et's begin by looking at the difference between osmotic and toxic preservation by reducing a complex process to a simple belt and braces concept.

Almost every school child of a certain age knows what osmosis means. It is the movement of water from a weak solution to a strong one. In other words it is the tendency of water to even out the concentration of dissolved substances. This movement of water can be used to stop living things, namely bacteria, from growing in food. If you put a solution that is stronger than the concentration inside a bacterium's cell in the food, then water will be forced out of the cell and into the food thus killing the bacterium. Osmotic disruption of microbes is the belt and we know that a belt is good enough to keep your trousers up, unless you are a gentleman of mature proportions.

The braces could perhaps be likened to the poisonous effect of saltpetre and its derivatives in the meat. These particles work by being toxic to bacteria and form a second line of defence; effectively the braces just in case the belt might snap under the strain.

The addition of saltpetre and sodium nitrite to foods has had some bad press in recent years. A lot of words have been written about nitrate in food and drinking water and studies have been made in many universities and hospitals that suggest nitrate is linked to a couple of problems, namely stomach cancer and blue baby syndrome.

Before a correct understanding of this question can be made we have to look at the particle that makes nitrate what it is.

Nitrate (No. 3) is an ion. This means it is a charged particle with one extra electron, and this gives it a certain amount of reactivity. Three oxygen atoms crowd the central nitrogen atom and on the whole it is fairly unstable. Some bacteria get their energy for life by converting No. 3 into nitrite, which has one less oxygen atom around it and is thus more stable. This process releases energy, but unfortunately for the bacteria nitrite (No. 2) is poisonous to them.

Interestingly, bacteria of this type live on our tongues, happily converting nitrates to nitrite in our saliva. This is a natural form of defence against dental decay and has probably been going on since our evolution.

Furthermore, the acidification of nitrite in the stomach creates nitric oxide, another chemical with further antibacterial qualities. This process has been our age-old protection against salmonella, which occurs in small quantities in the environment. People only succumb when their systems are overwhelmed with the bacteria from an infected food source.

Blue baby syndrome occurs when nitrite causes the oxidation of the iron centre of the haemoglobin. The blood cell then cannot acquire oxygen and if enough cells are affected the baby turns blue and can die. Studies have found this to be related to the production of nitric oxide/nitrite in the stomach which provides a natural defence to a major bout of gastroenteritis and not from the relatively tiny amount of nitrite ingested either in food or water. Babies should not be eating cured products, and in any case, the amount of nitrate/nitrite consumed would not be sufficient to cause this problem.

The cancer implications of nitrate/nitrite are more difficult to discuss. A number of studies have shown that nitrate/nitrite is converted into n-nitroso compounds, organic molecules which are given the designation NOS. It is these compounds that have been implicated as possible carcinogens.

Studies in the US and the UK have shown that the amount of these substances in cured food is not a cause for concern. Victorians used to add a lot more saltpetre than would be allowed today. Some Georgian fish recipes call for an initial pickling in salt and then a secondary storing in equal quantities of saltpetre and sugar. International agreements have restricted the amount of nitrate/nitrite permitted in food to a very low level.

Since the 1930s the incidence of stomach cancer has actually reduced and this is partly because we eat more refrigerated and fresh foods which are low in nitrate/nitrite and the actual amount of these substances has been controlled.

To put the problem into perspective, spinach grown naturally and organically in the garden can accumulate more nitrates in its leaves than would be allowed as an additive. This doesn't mean spinach is in itself dangerous. In fact we should eat it in abundance. Popeye will confirm this!

Nitrate/nitrite preservatives in food are safe in two circumstances. Firstly, there is not as much in modern cured food as in that consumed a hundred years ago and secondly, the amount of cured food we eat is considerably less than our grandparents would have eaten, a lot of food now being either frozen or fresh.

Throughout this book the recipes and procedures are written for curing salt. This has the appropriate legal amount of nitrate/nitrite.

It is much better to keep people safe from botulism than to leave out the chemicals which secure the safety of our food. If you are curing something that has to rely on the cure and is to be kept for a long time, make sure it has the appropriate amount of nitrate/nitrite. Simply use curing salt.

It is possible, however, to use ordinary kitchen salt for those foods you eat on a regular basis and leave out the saltpetre. Making green bacon without saltpetre will drastically reduce the nitrate/nitrite portion of your diet. Bacon never lasts that long because we eat it so quickly (well I do at least!) and can be cured so easily without saltpetre. It's called green bacon because it's actually greyish. It's only ever actually green in colour when it is off!

But do not be under any misunderstanding; botulism will kill you, and more people with you, than any increased risk of cancer should saltpetre and/or nitrite be omitted from the curing process.

Why saltpetre is a good preservative

The chemical reaction for nitrate to nitrite, as we have seen, is a natural process used by bacteria and other organisms. The great advantage, coincidentally, of using these ions as a preservative is that they are highly soluble. They are mobile and travel quickly to the depths of the meat. In order to help this, the use of a brine pump will make sure that thick pieces of food are correctly cured in the centre.

A word about salt

There is plenty of evidence that connects salt with high blood pressure, strokes and heart attacks. The current daily recommended intake of salt is 6g per day and an average portion of bacon will contain around 2.5g - 3g.

In order to reduce the amount of salt in bacon, soak it in water for ten minutes and dry it off with a towel before cooking. This will take around half the salt from the portion, and the bacon will still taste good. Do not be tempted to cure food with low sodium salt. If you wish to cut down your salt intake do it by eating salty foods less regularly and washing the salt out of the food before you cook it.

Similarly, do not use old-fashioned recipes for curing; even those devised in the last fifty years call for amounts of salt and saltpetre in ratios far too high for modern consumption. Always refer the quantities in old cookery books to modern literature.

Another way of lowering the salt in bacon is to cut down on the sugar in the cure. This sounds silly, but let me explain. The sugar is used to counteract the saltiness of the cure, and the food will taste saltier at lower concentrations. In other words you can salt the meat for a shorter time, and then use it quickly, not storing it for a long period.

Low salt bacon

Modern life calls for alternative ways of dealing with traditional food where salt is concerned. At present we do not have to rely on salt for preserving meat. It can be stored perfectly well in the freezer. The single problem is sourcing meat of a satisfactory freshness and quality. In my home town there used to be a hundred or so butchers. Now there is not even one. All of them could have provided the ideal product for curing but they have all gone out of business due to present day unfair competition with the larger national stores. You will often find that your only small local outlet now provides only frozen meat which is not appropriate for curing.

With this in mind I have experimented with producing homemade low salt bacon, which will work with thawed meat to make an acceptable product. You must, however, bear in mind that this product can only be kept for up to five days in the fridge and it must not be refrozen!

You will need a good slicer or, alternatively, if you still have one, get your local butcher to slice it for you. If the meat can be sliced while frozen it will be easier. Do be careful when slicing meat. If it suddenly turns red you know you have cut your finger.

Choose 500g of pork of any cut you prefer. Loin makes good bacon, but I prefer belly for a very special reason; the salt is only absorbed in the meat, so you only need add it to the meaty bits.

What you should have is twenty or so slices of pork, placed on a tray or large plate. Weight out 7.5g of salt (one and a half level teaspoons) and lightly sprinkle this over all the meat. An alternative way of doing this is to evenly spread half the salt in a roasting tin or large tray and to simply lay the thawed meat on it, sprinkling the rest of the salt over the top. Cover it with cling film and leave it for 24 hours in the refrigerator. As 7.5g spread over 500g of meat is only 1.5%, the salt content is much lower than usual.

Once this has settled, remove the cling film and pour off any liquor that has formed. It is unlikely there will be much. Give each piece a rub to ensure the salt is worked in and then you can add a secondary flavour. I like sugar, honey and smoke. Simply sprinkle the bacon with a very light dusting of sugar and leave it overnight. Alternatively, drizzle it with honey and hot smoke.

This product will not last long, not least because it is delicious and gets eaten quickly. A very large portion contains around 1.5g of salt and the flavour is very good. There is no need to add any saltpetre because the product is only intended to last a few days at most.

Fry it and you will be amazed that it is so easy to do. It tastes extremely good and it costs about one third of the cost of bought bacon. And you will have made it by hand; your hands, your food!

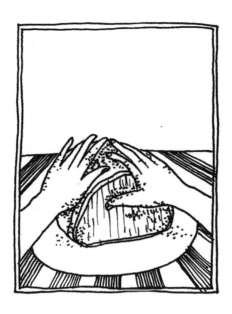

Chapter Four
Getting Started With Curing

The fundamental question you need to ask yourself is this. Are you curing for flavour or for preservation? This is a question we will visit again in relation to smoking, and has been recognised for a long time. Mrs. Beeton's recipe for Hunter's Beef has the following as an introduction:

"In salting or pickling beef or pork for family consumption, it not being generally required to be kept for a great length of time, a less quantity of salt and a larger quantity of other matters more adapted to retain mellowness in meat, may be employed, which could not be adopted by the curer of the immense quantities of meat required to be preserved for victualling the shipping of this maritime country".

No wonder they were called Salty Sea Dogs! It is possible to cure anything with less salt than is needed to actually preserve it beyond a couple of weeks. Usually the salting required to completely preserve meat will also contain in the associated recipe, an instruction to wash out the excess salt to improve the flavour as a part of the cooking process.

Mrs. Beeton also made the point that sugar preserves without changing the quality of the meat fibres and results in an altogether mellower and succulent product, with a better texture. Many cures have a 20% sweet content, either sugar or honey, but we have already gone into the reasons why sugar is not by itself a satisfactory preserver of meat.

Maynard Davies, author of a fantastic book called 'Maynard - Adventures of a Bacon Curer', said that to start curing you need washable walls. Not because you are going to cover them with the blood of terrified animals, but because the curing process needs cleanliness and a perfect hygienic fastidiousness. This is the most important lesson to be learned from this book. The rest is easy. In fact you will be amazed at how easy curing can be and you will probably be left looking at it and thinking that there must be more to it than this!

Ingredients

Curing salt is not the same as cooking or kitchen salt. What is often sold as curing salt is a variation of Prague powder. This is a pre-mixed product of saltpetre and kitchen salt. Another quicker acting version of Prague powder (known as Prague powder #2) contains sodium nitrate.

Read the instructions on your product carefully. For example, if you dilute the percentage of nitrite in the mix by adding other ingredients, the cure will not work so well. It all gets a bit messy and you end up trying to divide 6.25% of 1.36 kilos of meat and you may eventually go mad. The answer is to stick to the instructions on the salt cure packet. Use curing salt in the same amounts specified for ordinary salt and you will not go far wrong.

There is a simple set of rules to follow when deciding whether to use curing salt or ordinary salt. Use curing salt for anything which is thick, which might be needed over a long period of time or will be given to others. Ordinary kitchen salt can be used when you do not intend to keep the product but plan to eat it as you produce it. Bacon for immediate consumption is perhaps a good example of when you can use ordinary salt.

Ordinary table salt is used a lot in curing; buy the product that does not contain iodine; this can radically alter flavours. Do not be tempted to use sea salt with a coarse crystal structure. In dry curing you need to have fine particles that are easily rubbed into every nook and cranny.

Be sure that you know exactly what you are buying, because you might inadvertently use one instead of the other.

Doing the egg test

When you add salt to water it dissolves, as we all know. If you put an un-boiled egg in to water it will sink, but if you keep on dissolving salt in the water it will eventually float. As soon as the egg floats it just happens to be exactly the right concentration for curing.

Sugar, either white or brown, is a fundamental part of the cure; the darker the colour, the smokier and richer the mix. Honey and molasses are also used for hams and bacon and not just for the cure.

Saltpetre is used for additional security in the cure. You can really only be sure of a botulism free product for the long-term storage of cured meat when the appropriate amount of saltpetre has been added. You only ever use a small amount, around 6 % of the final amount of salt in the mix, and in order to maintain accuracy it is best to make up a lot of cure or alternatively to buy a commercial mixture. (At the risk of being boring: buy curing salt. Look in the resources section for a supplier.)

Spices and peppers of all kinds are called for in various recipes, including things like garlic salt. You do not need to worry about the salt content of these because they are used in small quantities.

I have a problem with garlic. I simply do not like the flavour of garlic salt or dried garlic granules. I get round this in two ways. For a very mild garlic flavour I simply rub a cut clove all around the meat. This has a dual purpose in that cut garlic gives off a chemical called allicin which is a very strong antibacterial agent.

For a stronger garlic flavour I grate some cloves but do not add it to the cure. Instead I rub this into the meat first and give it a couple of hours in the fridge to dry. Then I use the cure and continue

the process. Try ransomes or wild garlic, often found growing in damp areas in May. It will prove a wonderful alternative.

Containers

You will need a variety of containers for all sorts of substances. They should be air tight, child proof and easily cleanable. If you make your own cures you will need a large sealable container. The marmalade industry uses white polythene tubs that carry eighty pounds, and there are plenty of equivalents in the Resources section.

Similarly, large sealable containers in which you can actually do the preserving can be made from good quality plastic, but there is something really pleasant about using crockery. We forget that crockery includes preserving dishes and not just plates, cups and saucers.

The recipe for overnight bacon uses a single container, but if you are preparing a ham you need somewhere to hang it. If you can afford the space, a fridge is the ideal spot. To my mind the kitchen rafters is probably the worst place to hang a ham because there will be inevitable changes in both temperature and humidity. A cool larder is much better and even a shed is OK, as long as it doesn't leak and the meat is well protected.

Scales

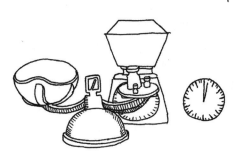

You really do need a good set of scales. Balance scales, those gorgeous brass affairs that old-fashioned kitchens have, are fine if they are a really good pair. Cheaper ones have difficulty in weighing out smaller quantities and usually the smallest weight of 5g does not even move the pan at all. It is important to be able to accurately weigh quantities less than 10g and if you are not able to do this with certainty you will need a new set of scales.

Mixing

Everyone can easily acquire a good set of mixing bowls. A good sized stock pot, however, is a different matter. If you are wet curing a ham as big as a butcher's arm then you need an appropriate pot! Mixing cures is an entirely different matter. Perhaps I am being pedantic but to my mind a quick flash around a bowl with a wooden spoon will not evenly mix a teaspoon full of one substance in a kilo of another. Imagine putting black powder into white powder. It will take a lot of beating to get them completely and evenly mixed.

I use a food processor to mix a small quantity with as much as my container will hold and then use this amount to mix into the rest of the ingredients. If I have to mix a teaspoon of one substance with a bucket full of salt I will mix a bowlful in the processor first, knowing that this is then completely mixed and then use this to mix with the larger amount. Needless to say this means you will also need a good quality mixer.

Cutting

A butcher's boning knife and the appropriate sharpener to go with it are really great tools.

Use a steel sharpener, not one of those irritating little sharpeners that people buy from the supermarket. If you go to your butcher he will teach you how to use it properly, particularly if you are buying some meat from him! One of the sad characteristics of modern life is that people do not know how important sharpness is in the kitchen because everything comes pre-sliced. If you are making sandwich ham you will need a good knife to cut out all the meat!

Along with this, to avoid making finger ham, you could buy a metal gauntlet for your non-cutting hand. You only need one because, try as you may, it is almost impossible to cut the hand that holds the knife.

Slicing

Not cutting your finger is probably the second most important reason for buying a slicer. The single most important reason is to get proper cuts of meat, particularly bacon, which is a serious pain to cut properly with a knife. I must say, however, that I have done this quite successfully for many years. You simply need a really good knife, but we have already mentioned that.

At the time of writing a good domestic slicer costs around £40.00 but you can find very good semi-industrial ones second hand for a similar amount.

Presses

Making sandwich meat from cuts needs a press. You could use a tube, a plate and a lot of tins, or the DIY experts among you might choose to rig something up with a G-clamp. Alternatively, you can buy a press that allows you to make professionally pressed meat.

Vacuum packing

Do you need a vacuum packing machine? Well, excluding the air and wrapping food in plastic does increase its shelf life. It is a sign of the times that you can buy a vacuum packing machine but not a canning machine. Fans of John Seymour will note that his descriptions of the can-o-matic are now relegated to history, in the UK at least. This has been superseded by the use of bottles with screw lids.

For most purposes vacuum packing is not really necessary, regardless of how good an idea it may be. There should be few reasons for keeping food for longer than the natural curing would allow because you just don't know if it's safe. Consequently simple every day packaging should meet the needs of most curers but if you really have set your heart on the acquisition of a vacuum packing machine please don't let me put the dampers on it.

There will doubtless be many people who disagree and who cook food in vacuum packed bags, thus preserving them for a very long time. We shall, however, concentrate on traditional curing and smoking, except in one instance: vacuum packaging is fantastic for storing smoked mackerel – kippers to you and me!

One further advantage of vacuum packing is the opportunity to cure in a vacuum-sealed bag. It is an excellent way of making bacon. You simply rub the cure into the meat and then vacuum seal. This keeps the process in its own environment, and it is easy to store.

Syringe or brine pump?

A lot of bad press, and quite rightly so, has come about because some unscrupulous retailers have been artificially increasing the weight of their meat by adding water to it.

However, home made cured meat is a different matter. If you are making boiled ham with a big piece of meat then simply relying on osmosis for the cure to get to the centre might not be good enough. It is perfectly acceptable to inject cure into the centre of the meat with a syringe to aid the curing process.

Disposable gloves

This is an excellent way of protecting your hands and maintaining cleanliness. They also allow you to work in the kitchen and avoid cross contamination with other foods, a particularly important factor in the curing process.

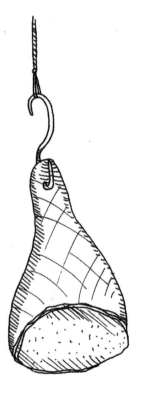

Butcher's hook

These are invaluable things to use for hanging meat. Use stainless steel because they do not impart any taint onto the meat. Do not forget to clean and sterilise them in boiling water, otherwise they simply become sources of infection.

Cures and cure recipes

There are lots of companies out there selling meat cures, already spiced with lots of recipes, some hot and spicy, others mild and easy on the tongue. You need to decide what you want from your curing. You might be providing meat in a self-sufficient way and consequently need an excellent cure. You might be making a product such as home cured bacon, and combining this with freezing you might be able to use a home made, nitrite free cure that will do an excellent job. There is, however, nothing wrong with buying your cures just as there is nothing wrong with making your own.

The various different types of cure are described in the last section of the book, and their use is outlined below. The idea of this section is to give you a general outline of what is possible, a layer of knowledge that will be added to later.

Basic green bacon cure

This bacon is not green, but nor is it pink either!

Green bacon cure has no saltpetre. It is simply a mixture of salt and sugar with at least 70% being salt. You can flavour this if you like with various additions.

These are some that have worked for me. You can, of course, choose any combination you like but do make the additions in total represent no more than 5% of the mixture by weight.

Bay   (finely chopped and up to 1% of the total weight)
Rosemary   (finely chopped and up to 3% of the total weight)
Pepper   (up to 1% of the total weight)
Mustard   (up to 1% of the total weight)
Mint   (finely chopped and up to 2% of the total weight)

Of course you can vary the type of cure by changing the type of sugar you use. Thick brown sugar will give a completely different flavour to that of refined white sugar. I usually give the coarse sugars a quick grinding in the pestle and mortar in an attempt to get all the crystals the same size.

How much to make

This obviously depends on how much you eat bacon and what sized sealable container you have to store it. I have found that making a kilo of this type of cure will last two or three small curing sessions. This works out at a few kilos of belly pork at a time, so I tend to make up a batch of that amount, but do make sure you label the container properly. I once made a batch of white pepper, salt and white sugar and someone mistook it for table salt with horrendous consequences.

Three Important Ground Rules

1. Make sure you know the food is safe to eat in the first place.(Could you cook it and eat it safely prior to curing? If not then no amount of curing will make it safe).

2. Stick to the recipes.

3. Don't experiment beyond your ability.

How to make simple bacon

There are a number of ways of using this type of cure and once you find one you really like it is quite possible you will not buy bacon again. The cuts of meat you use will vary, but this works very well for a kilo of belly pork.

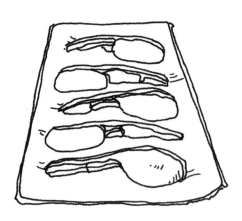

Method 1: The overnight blast.

This is for making bacon that will last no longer than a week and is more flavouring than anything else, but it certainly works a treat.

Wash everything!

Place your belly pork into a container that has a layer of cure in the bottom. Rub the cure into the meat, covering all the surfaces and then cover the whole of the meat with cure. Seal the container and place it in the refrigerator until the morning.

The container will be half full of liquor, which should be discarded, the meat washed of all cure and then tested. It will be slightly 'porkish' in colour, not pink. Cut a piece off and fry it. If it tastes right then simply slice it up and go hunt for the eggs!

Method 2: The rub it in method

This way you take enough of your cure to generously cover just the meat, and rub it in all over. Be quite vigorous with this process and force the cure into the flesh. Once it has been well rubbed, place it in a dish which you then seal with cling film and leave it overnight. In the morning you need to pour off the liquor and repeat the process. You then repeat this for 5 days, after which you should test your bacon.

In both cases the skin of the pork changes consistency, as does the meat. Those of us who are old enough will remember bacon rind, which comes from the skin. This is old fashioned bacon indeed!

So why test the meat?

First of all, it might just be too salty for your liking. The answer is then to soak it in water and retest it. The thickness of meat also varies so look at the inside of your product to be sure the process has affected it. You can always lengthen the time a little and then test the product again. Salted meat will keep well while it is salty so you can always soak it just prior to cooking.

Cure it in the refrigerator at around 2°C and label the container so you know exactly when the meat was cured and how old it is. Make sure that you get the freshest meat you can and always cook bacon made in this way.

Other bacon cures

There are a large number of bacon cures that are sold by companies, each of them is great value and all will be completely safe provided you stick to the manufacturer's instructions, which usually involve a few days of curing.

If you are new to curing, this is an excellent way to start. The processes generally involve rubbing cure into the meat and storing it for the prescribed period. Sometimes this is measured in days per weight, or some recipes call for days per unit length for curing something like a large piece of belly pork.

Cure travels by osmosis and diffusion to penetrate the meat. It dissolves in water in the muscle, not the fat of the, well, fat. The skin is almost impenetrable. It is best to use most of the cure on the muscle and either to cut off excess fat or make sure the cure is really working inside the fat layer by slicing small areas and adding cure.

In making bacon, think thickness. A piece of belly is quite thin, so the cure can penetrate right up to the fat quite easily.

Corned Beef Cure

We buy corned beef in tins and have been used to the flavour for more than two generations. However, home made corned beef is so different. The word 'corned' is Old English for 'crumb' and can refer to any seed as well as the way salt collects into a crumb when it is used in a dry cure. This is an excellent way of storing a piece of beef in a refrigerator or cool place and once cured the meat will last for several months. It must, however, be cooked before eating.

The recipe for sufficient cure to make 5 kilos of corned beef (not as much as it sounds!) is as follows:

Choose a cut that is not fatty. The greater the fat, the harder it is to cure. Remove any excess fat. You will then require the following ingredients:

500g salt
75g of sugar
1 tbsp of cracked pepper corns
1 tsp of paprika
1 tsp of finely chopped sage
1 tsp of crushed bay leaf
2 tsp of allspice

Now clean everything.

Next mix all the ingredients in a bowl thoroughly to make sure they are completely evenly combined. It will be better if you can do the next stage inside a clear sealable plastic bag, but it works just as well wrapped in cling film.

Vigorously rub the cure around all the surfaces of the meat, wasting none. Put some of the cure onto some cling film; enough to wrap the meat. Then place the rubbed beef on the film and wrap it up while placing excess cure all around. You are looking to make a parcel of beef with cure evenly all around it, wrapped in cling film.

Place it in a container and put it in the refrigerator.

Massage the meat through the film every day for 2 weeks, turning the meat over every day too. Repeat this for a fortnight and then you may simply leave it like this in the cool for several months.

You do not need 5 kg of salted beef, so cut off the amount you need to use and rewrap the beef. It needs to be soaked in several changes of water for 2 days prior to cooking.

This meat is not full of blood and as such is more difficult to cook. Boiling it in water until the meat is tender is probably the best method; you can use a meat thermometer to make sure the very centre has reached 75°C for at least 15 minutes.

Boiled or roast ham

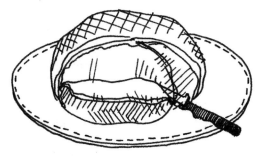

A boiled ham, or sandwich ham, is easy to make and this recipe calls for pickling spice, which is easily made at home from this generic recipe. I tend to leave out the cloves because they remind me of the dentist.

Give them a good working with the pestle so that the cinnamon stick can be handled with a spoon and the flavours leach out. Store the mixture in an airtight container.

The cure makes a gallon, or 4.5 litres, and you do not need all of this for a ham, so you need a good sealable container for the excess cure mix.

Ingredients for boiled or roast ham

2 bay leaves

2 tbsp of mustard seed

2 tsp of black peppercorns

2 tsp of whole cloves

1 tbsp of allspice

1 tsp of ground ginger

1 tsp of cardamom seeds

1 cinnamon stick

The essential ingredient is curing salt with nitrate & nitrite.

1 kg of curing salt
4.5 litres (1 gallon) of water
125g of sugar
1 tbsp of the pickle spices as above

The meat is probably best as a lean pork loin, or a boned leg. If you do not have your own pig to slaughter, buy from a proper butcher who can guarantee the meat has not been frozen.

Cool the cure by keeping it in a cold fridge overnight and ensure that the brine remains in a cool place throughout the process. I use a plastic bucket with a sealable lid in which to do the curing, which takes around 5 days. You can inject the cure into the centre of the meat if you like.

Once this is complete it is time to cook your ham. There are a number of recipes for this. Some place the ham in boiling water and cook it for an hour. You can cook it in the oven in water, or you can roast it with a honey topping. There are many recipes in the back of the book, including slicing and frying it with eggs!

In all cooking of cured meat products I would advocate the use of a meat thermometer whereby you can guarantee that the centre of the meat has been heated to 75°C for at least 15 minutes.

Pressed tongue

An ox tongue is a huge piece of meat, impossible to eat quickly enough and consequently it has to be preserved if it is to last. The most common way of doing this is in a curing salt solution, in which the tongue must stand for a week before boiling.

Following this the tongue can be frozen to keep it and when you come to use it, soak it in water for a couple of days.

The tongue needs to be simmered for four hours after soaking. After a while a scum will form. This needs to be removed before a series of vegetables are added to the stock. When cooked the skin is removed and the rough bits are trimmed from the remainder. Force the tongue into a baking tin so you can only just get it in place and put a plate on it. Press it with a heavy weight. Many recipes chose to set it in gelatine. I am told it tastes good sliced thinly on sandwiches, though I have to confess I can't bear it myself.

Ham: the dry option

The British climate has not been all that kind to the would-be air dryer of meat. This is why we are more famous in this country for short-lived wet sausages than for those air-finished salamis which come from abroad. However, York is as famous for ham as Bayonne or Parma, and it is quite possible to make your own, provided you stick to the rules.

The basic idea behind air-dried ham is that it is completely cured, inside and out, and then matured. The meat can then be sliced very thinly, cooked whole or sliced to add to all kinds of dishes. This is only one of several methods for making a ham described in the recipe section.

It is probably best to buy a mix if you are going to dry cure a ham. Of course, you must only treat the very freshest of meat, and remove any excess skin and fat which might hinder the cure's process. The basic idea is to rub in the cure over all the meat. It is probably best if the meat is also de-boned.

Then wrap it in cling film, adding more cure all around and leave it in the fridge for three weeks. Then remove the meat and wash it. Repeat the above process for a second three weeks and then remove and wash it as before. Cover the whole ham in a piece of stockinette and hang it in a cool dry room for at least a month, possibly three. The relative humidity should be less than 60% and the temperature should be cool, around 12°C.

Ham: the wet option

Pickled hams are easier to make. The cure is dissolved in water and consists of curing salt, spices etc. (do the egg test). The ham is soaked for a week to ten days. It should be held under the cure by a wooden board and weighted down otherwise it tends to float. The ham should be turned in the pickle each day to ensure an even process. You should be able to tell by your nose if the ham is going off.

The inside of the ham is injected with the same cure using a brine pump. A large ham can have the cure pumped right into the centre of the meat, known as the cushion; the fatless side, where the bone is visible. This will make for a really safe product.

Once the curing time has ended (a week for a small ham, ten days for a large one) the ham is removed, washed, wrapped in stockinette and hung as for a dry cured ham.

Ham Shank

This is a serious delicacy of the northern climes of the UK. It is basically a foreleg shin of pork that has been cured. There is a lot of skin and fat on the cut and since the only part of a pig that cannot be eaten is the squeal, this material is integral to the dish. You can use the same cure as for the boiled ham and it can be injected behind the skin, while the rest of the joint can be cured for five days as above.

The shank is then boiled in a large pot and the gelatinous material from the bone and knuckle forms something of a coating. By the same process, if roasted the salt reacts with the fat under heat and makes superb crackling.

Of course it goes without saying that since these cuts are eaten right away you can cure them without saltpetre. A French variation covers them with fat to make a confit to preserve them a little longer.

The same generic cure can also be used for bacon ribs. This product has been a staple of the poor of the country for many hundreds of years. Served with cabbage it is perhaps a messy food for many of today's palates, and perhaps Chinese style spare ribs would suit many more people. Cured pigs' ribs are soaked for three days in the generic cure used for boiled ham and then hung, wrapped in muslin. They can also be sealed in fat to protect them further. A cured sheet of ribs will last for a month. They must be boiled before eating.

Brawn

They say 'brains before brawn' but brawn probably has some brains in it. Well, a residual amount anyway! This really is the Hammer House of Horrors of the kitchen.

I find that if you treat this process clinically and stick to clean techniques, making a fresh and clean looking liquor and concentrating mentally on producing as clear a product as possible, then it is just about possible for a modern twentieth century human to do this job at home. Remember, any abhorrence is all in the mind!

Brawn is usually the pickled head meat of a pig, but there are similar recipes for rabbit and beef brawn as well as others. However, nothing works better than pork.

The most important prerequisite for this dish, or rather the bits that can turn it into a complete disaster, are the hairs, which have to be removed with a razor. No one likes a moustache sandwich!

First of all, the head should be soaked for around three to five days in a brine made from curing salt with the correct amount of saltpetre. Some old recipes call for the head to be pickled in ordinary salt and then to be re-treated with saltpetre and sugar, but we do not use such high quantities these days.

Once the head is pickled it is then boiled for hours and hours until the meat simply falls off the bone. You might wish to remove a large quantity of the skin and the pan will contain bits of teeth and all sorts of grizzly things. As the liquor boils, remove any scum that collects on the surface. See also the recipe for Pig Cheek Bacon in Chapter 12.

Collect the meat from the rest of the boiling and discard everything except the liquor that you are going to boil down so that it will eventually set as a jelly. Adding a couple of trotters to the pot can help this.

Your liquor will be all the clearer if you are fastidious about scooping away any scum as it appears. Some recipes call for the meat to be ground and then heated again in vinegar, but chopping it finely works just as well.

Add the meat to skim and strain the liquor, preferably through a muslin bag then add the meat to the liquor in a glass dish and set a very hot plate on the top which has been liberally cleaned in boiling water. Allow it to cool and then put it in the fridge.

Most recipes call for the brawn to be left for a week. They might say this is to allow the flavours to develop. I firmly believe it is to give you a chance to forget the gastronomic nightmare of messing about with an animal's severed head.

Sandwich meat

As per the ham shank, you can cure many different cuts of meat, particularly trotters, in the same manner. Boil them and, once cooked, remove the lean meat from the skin and fat. You should have a good jelly left after the boiling.

Press the meat in a large dish or a loaf tin with a lid or a specially purchased press and carefully top it up with jelly. This creates the very best sandwich ham you could imagine. The same principle goes for beef and chicken, although you should not really salt chicken too heavily.

Salisbury meat

Everyone thinks that hamburgers were invented as a fast food or come out of the freezer, but they were originally a way of making small cuts of meat such as oxtail, low shin and cheek last a week. If you believe the various claims for the invention of the hamburger it seems to be something that has been around for a hundred or so years. Hamburger Charlie was one of the claimants to having invented the hamburger when he simply flattened a meatball. The term Salisbury meat came about during the First World War. The Americans, who are not good at hiding their feelings, changed the name of the hamburger to Salisbury meat to remove any Germanic connection.

Hamburgers do not contain any ham. They are a combination of ground beef, salt, perhaps a little cereal and that's it although some are spiced. They will keep for a week if the salt content is around 1.5%, especially if refrigerated. Of course they will also freeze well, and they will cook quickly if the meat is well ground.

The inclusion of the hamburger in this book shows that most of our cuisine, particularly in relation to meat, has evolved as a result of the need for two things: to improve the palatability of certain cuts and to improve its keeping qualities. Today, however, we make luxury hamburgers from fresh steak, in my own view a complete waste of money and way beyond the remit of this book.

To make 20 decent hamburgers you will need 2kg of the cheapest but freshest beef; skirt, shin or cheek and 30g of salt. Simply whiz it all up in the food processor, grind it with the grinder or, if you are completely hand powered, pound away at it in the mortar, mixing the salt thoroughly and evenly. You can then add a dessert spoon of any of the following:

Tomato puree
Ground garlic
Black pepper (only a teaspoon)
Mint leaves (chopped)
Thyme
Coriander seeds (only a teaspoon)

Avoid at all costs the temptation to 'bind' the burgers with egg, which will certainly go off more quickly than the meat.

You can then use a pastry cutter to make the burgers, simply piling them together, each one separated from its neighbour by a sheet of greaseproof paper. Finally seal them in a bag and either refrigerate or freeze them.

Dried beef

This is known as jerky in the United States where it is very popular. It is a highly salted product, usually smoked (we look at smoking later!) and air dried. It makes an excellent food for people who are on long distance walks because it is light, easily transportable and highly nutritious.

The recipes probably work equally well for venison and rabbit because they are a much leaner meat, more amenable to curing. It is also possible to dry the meat once cured and then to smoke it in a hot smoker before eating, thus cooking the meat as well as smoking it.

It is even possible to make a hamburger in a long strip and then dry it in the oven, but most recipes call for whole muscle, no 'fat' thin cuts of meat. The pieces of meat need to be 5mm thick, so do use a slicer.

You can buy specially prepared jerky spiced curing salt. If you are making your own, use curing salt instead of table salt and add a few spices. Add 2g of cracked black pepper, crushed garlic, sage, rosemary or onion to 100g of curing salt and rub the mix into the strips of meat. Be generous, around a teaspoon to a pound of meat, and put it into a container which should be refrigerated.

You can dry the meat in a drying cupboard, or in a low oven as though you were making meringues. It is ready when the meat becomes difficult to bend but has not yet become brittle. The meat will keep for a couple of months and can be eaten by soaking it in water or if you prefer you can eat it once smoked though I prefer to cook it.

Pies

People overlook the fact that a pie is a way of preserving its contents as well as making something nice to eat. When it comes to the king of pies, the pork pie, the meat is almost any cut you like, ground and mixed with salt and spices. The pastry acts as a way of protecting the cooked contents, and as the jelly sets inside the pie, the meat is completely sealed.

Hot water crust pastry is heavily laden with fat, forming an effective airtight seal, and bacteria find growing in fat particularly difficult, so a well cooked pie can last for over a week. However, once the pie is cut, it will begin to deteriorate very quickly.

Chicken

We have a history of fresh chicken in the UK. The word chicken is Anglo Saxon and is plural, so it would be wrong to refer to chickens. We do not have a history of preserving chicken, except for one single and most wonderful product; pressed salted jellied chicken.

It is not possible to make this product in the same way as canned salted chicken, but you can have a close approximation by roasting your chicken in the normal way (you can boil it if you prefer) and using the breast as a meal, but saving the other meat; the skirt, oysters, wing and underside. After having stripped your carcass, spread the meat onto a sterile plate and sprinkle it with salt at the rate of half a flat teaspoon to every 100 g of meat. Sprinkle it so that the salt is evenly applied and then press the meat into a terrine.

Place the carcass into a small amount of water in a lidded pan and simmer it for at least an hour. Then strain the liquid and reduce it until it is a quarter of its original volume. You can cool a small portion to see if it sets naturally, or alternatively you can add a piece of gelatine and a quarter of a teaspoon of salt.

Pour the liquid into the terrine and allow it to set. Due to all the concerns about chicken, and even though everything has been sterilised and boiled to death, I still only keep this for three days, but oh what sandwiches it makes!

Eggs

Eggs are preserved in the later summer and autumn in readiness for the winter. Modern egg producers maintain laying stocks by artificially manipulating the length of the day by using appropriate lighting regimes. However, this is not possible for a small flock or the smallholder.

We can preserve eggs in a number of ways. Egg shells are actually perforated by lots of holes so the growing chick can breathe and this is the route for microbes to get into the egg. If you can block up these holes the eggs will last a long time, possibly up to a year.

A 10% solution of water glass (sodium silicate) does this job very well. You must choose only the very best eggs, clean and embryo free (do candle them first!). They must be only a couple of days old and not cracked. Do not try to preserve bought eggs from the supermarket; they might be as much as a month old.

Pickling eggs is a different matter. They must be very hard boiled and plunged into ice water. From this the eggs are pickled in vinegar that has been treated with spices. Pickled eggs will last for a year with little difficulty, though I have no personal experience of them lasting more than a month

Chapter Five
Curing Fish

A moonraker is a poacher who, after having caught his booty, then puts it into a sack and throws it into the village pond. Perhaps this is the reason why so many villages have ponds! When the gamekeepers are no longer searching for him he can then 'rake the moon,' that is to say, go back at night and recover his rotting carcasses of meat or fish from the moonlit pond.

In bygone times most village ponds were so full of illegal salmon and trout that there was consequently a need to eat it quickly. There are no peasant recipes recorded to preserve such royal fish. We do have smoked salmon and trout which are very much a delicacy but would have been so prohibitively expensive that only the rich could afford them (it was their fish anyway). For this reason there is not much history relating to the preserving of freshwater fish, save elvers and eels.

The majority of cured fish are caught in the sea. The curing was not just to make them last a long time, but really to make them last any time at all. A herring caught one day can be inedible the next, and this certainly goes for mackerel. Large fishing boats have plenty of ice on board, and factory ships have refrigeration plants to process and freeze the little fishes in their millions.

In days gone by the only real way of transporting fish was under salt. It was only the arrival of the railway which brought fresh fish to the centre of cities for the first time, and since then we only have cured fish for the additional flavours it offers.

To the best of my knowledge there is actually nothing to stop a person going to the sea and salting down a whole load of inshore fish then and there on the beach. Similarly, there are millions of creatures from crabs to shrimps that we can pot and salt and cure. British seafood is the very finest in the world and instead of turning our noses up at it we should instead be getting stuck in. It is a never-ending puzzlement to me that non-British EU trawlers buy up British quotas for fishing and get the best we have to offer. Of the millions of tons of fish landed from our waters, only a fraction is destined for our own kitchens. This is truly a national disaster of immense proportions.

A fishy beef

If this was a political book there would follow a tirade on how the ruling classes, from 1067 onwards, conspired to enslave the population and, after starving them to death during the years of the Norman conquest, they then proceeded to make it impossible for men to catch the fish that swam in their rivers, the shellfish that lived on their shores or the fish that swam in their seas. This state of affairs has worsened every decade until now when the ordinary Briton does not even own the rain that falls on his head.

But it is essentially a cookery book and I shall say only this. You can barely catch fish economically in rivers and eat them these days because they probably belong to some landlord or other, and to pull them out will cost you a small fortune in fees. I caught a trout which actually cost me £30! I could have bought 6 for that! The very same desire to profit from our land has led to the rivers being heavily polluted which means that if the water is clean you can't fish it without paying a fortune and if it's not clean you wouldn't want to. Such is life.

Preparing fish

First, be sure that the fish is fresh and that you are quite aware of its origin, and consequently its fitness for consumption. This especially applies to freshwater fish. You can catch trout in the River Tame, but they are so full of mercury that you might endanger your life if you eat them.

Please, fisherman, kill the animal before removing the hook if at all possible. It is enough that the animal has died for our dinner, so please minimise its suffering. If you are new to fishing you kill a fish with a Priest. Some Pope or other forbade priests from defending themselves with a blade so a startling array of cudgels appeared to do the job more gruesomely. The remnant of this equipment is a fisherman's Priest; something with which to deliver the last rights.

Be careful with filter feeders. Bivalve molluscs must be alive before cooking them. They are usually closed or slightly closed and if you give them a tap they will shut tight. No amount of preserving will make them edible if they are off. If you are collecting limpets, give them a kick and make sure they respond but you will have to look carefully. Shrimps are best boiled at the beach, or as near to it as possible.

De-scale your fish by roughly scraping the skin with a knife but if you have bought it from a supermarket, do not preserve it unless you intend to eat it the same day. Put the heads and fins in the stockpot and get as much goodness from them as you can. If you respect the fact that these were once living creatures, you will be respecting the planet and yourself too. Do not make fish stock from anything that comes from inside the fish.

Fish stock

This is a way of preserving every last drop of goodness from your catch. You eventually will only throw away the tasteless hulk of the bones and flesh. The stock can be frozen, but will keep if stored in a cool larder.

Mix the ingredients and bring them to the boil. Then simmer them for 30 minutes and pass the liquid through a muslin bag to strain it. Finally, let it cool.

Freshwater fish

Jellied eels

This was a popular dish that was highly favoured in Southern England. Originally it only applied to eels which, when boiled with their bones intact, produced a jelly. The jelly would preserve the fish for about a week, particularly if salted. Nutmeg is used in most recipes.

These days the animal has to be fresh, gutted and boned, then cleaned with lemon juice. A little nutmeg is then added.

Cut the eel into four-inch strips, roll it with the skin outermost and tie it with string before you boil them in a liquor made from fish stock or water with a little chopped onion and celery. When the fish is cooked, around 20 minutes later, put enough gelatine into the strained liquor and when it has dissolved, pour it over the fish. Then allow it to cool before eating it.

Freshwater fish preserved in jelly

Today the very same dish can be made with any edible freshwater fish, particularly trout, pike and zander, if gelatine is used. Remember that a lot of freshwater fish are actually little better to eat than a pincushion, perch and roach being the worst offenders. You will have to scrape the meat away with a fork and then make a jelly for the flesh like a confit, served in a ramekin, covered all over in jelly. It is almost an alternative version of potted fish, which uses butter.

Some recipes call for simply reducing the stock to such an extent that it sets naturally. Tudor recipes call for the addition of saffron to the stock.

Freshwater fish pickle

Making a pickle for fish involves boiling them in vinegar and spices, but this does not completely preserve them. They have to be cleaned and gutted as soon as possible after being caught and then laid down to salt, which is the preservative.

Fillet and salt each piece, piling them into a container. They should be kept like this for a week. Then wash off the salt and prepare your

Ingredients for Fish Stock

White fish with all the trimmings weighing around a pound altogether

A peeled onion cut in half

A carrot, washed and cut into large pieces

1 dessertspoon of salt

1 tbsp of lemon juice

1 litre of water

pickle mix.

Bring the liquids, onions and celery to the boil and add your washed fish. Cook it for 15 minutes. This amount of liquid is enough for 5 kilos of fish.

Then prepare your jars and add the fish, topping them up with the pickle. Seal them immediately and allow them to cool. They will keep in the refrigerator for two months.

Salt-water fish

In this chapter we are looking only at the preservation of the fish. The production of various smoked fish will be dealt with in a later chapter so please be patient.

If you take a pile of fish whole and leave them in a big bucket, they will begin to smell. After a week or so the intestines will burst open and their contents will speed up the decomposition of the flesh. A handful of salt will kill any bacteria and after three months the resulting goo can be bottled and used as a condiment for soups and other dishes. Well, that's what the ancient Romans thought anyway; they called it garum. Personally I wouldn't touch it with a barge pole.

Essentially, however, salting fish is still the same process except that the fish are gutted and then covered in salt, both inside and out. An excess of salt is used and the fish are piled one on top of another until you have a barrel of them. When I go fishing I like to kill and clean the fish on the beach and salt them straight away. After a while the flesh turns yellow and hardens.

The fish need to be soaked for 24 hours in several changes of water before cooking. They are quite acceptable fried or baked or especially used as an ingredient on a pizza or in a more traditional fisherman's pie. If you are careful you can even get good-sized fillets.

This is the first step you will take prior to smoking all fish. The smoke is there really only to improve the flavour and as a way of drying the fish still further. The single absolute method of preservation for smoked fish is the use of salt.

Brine preserved fish

The use of brine instead of dry salt is important for fish like salmon, particularly if it is to be smoked. The egg test provides the correct concentration of salt to use. If you are going to make cool smoked salmon where the product will be eaten raw, use curing salt, which is not normally necessary for fish. Do remember that if you are eating raw fish, freeze it once the curing process is complete. This will guarantee that any parasites are killed. The fish will need to be gutted in the same way as for dry salted fish.

You can preserve your own salmon in brine by cutting fillets across the bone and soaking them in a brine solution for three days. Then

A Standard Pickle Mix

500ml of water

4 litres of vinegar

2 onions, peeled and quartered

2 sticks of celery, chopped

You can also add bay leaves, sliced lemons and even sliced onions or sliced salad onions.

bring it to the boil in a pan with a 60% solution of brine (as diluted using a brine solution made by using the egg test). Once the flesh has been completely cooked, store them in sterile Kilner jars topped up with the strained, diluted brine. Fish preserved in this manner should last for a month.

Similarly, cooked fish can be stored in oil. It has to be thoroughly salted or brined beforehand, and cooked and allowed to cool a little before oiling.

Pickled fish uses exactly the same pickle mixture as for pickled meats or eggs to soak the fish, usually herring. It is brined and salted first, then brought to the boil in a vinegar solution spiced with various flavours from capers to onions. The fish has usually been boned and then rolled, the rolled shape held together with a toothpick. This is precisely how rollmops are made.

Potted Shrimp

It was only recently that I found out you could still buy shrimping nets. This was a fascination of seaside holidays for many decades; off you would go and see if you could get a net full of flashing crustaceans. Really posh people used to have special little methylated spirit burners to boil the catch up in seawater. Nothing beats seafood cooked this way, and indeed you have to boil them within minutes of catching or else they will go bad.

Potted shrimp is a great way of keeping the excess animals you cannot eat for a week. Also, this is the only dish you can reasonably make from frozen shrimps and prawns. Usually these creatures are vacuumed from the sea, cleaned, cooked and frozen in a single operation and consequently they are very fresh.

Fresh shrimps are brought to the boil and simmered for three minutes. They should then have the legs and shell removed before being placed in hot ramekin dishes. A mixture of hot butter and nutmeg is poured into the dish, right up to the top. Pour it slowly and make sure that all the air spaces are filled. Then allow it to cool and set.

Molluscs

Somehow I have to get over the idea that I am eating a slug. The smell of cockles in vinegar soon dispels this aberration and there is nothing more wholesome. "Cockles, winkles, alive, alive 'O" are first cooked in boiling brine. They are easy to flick out of their open shells into the boiling brine for a few seconds. Do make sure that you discard any shells already open before cooking. They can then be ladled into sterile jars and topped up with hot brine. Boiling spiced pickling vinegar can be used as an alternative if preferred.

Do make sure that you discard any shells already open before cooking.

Chapter Six
Getting Started With Smoking

Right from the start you have to make a decision about smoking; will it be hot or cold? They do not produce the same product but you do end up with something really tasty with both.

Cold smoking is the traditional way of drying food while at the same time imparting a smoked flavour. It does not dry the food sufficiently to preserve it completely. All smoked products will first have been salted or cured in one way or another. This is important to remember because some smoked food still needs to be cooked before it is eaten.

Cold Smoking

Cold smoking is a four-stage process consisting of curing, drying, smoking and storing. The drying process allows the product to form what is known as a pellicle which is a hardened outer skin that allows the smoke to adhere and then to penetrate into the product.

Cold smoking separates the smoke from the source of heat, though the air is still quite warm, often around 25°C. This is usually achieved by sending the smoke through a pipe before it reaches the smoking chamber. You can make your own smoker using an old fridge and some ducting from a stove some two metres away.

You can also buy a smoke generator which burns compressed briquettes of wood and can be ducted into the main compartment of a fridge. Just as easy, though, is setting a hook high in a chimney if you are lucky enough to have one or going the whole hog and buying a complete smoking machine. You will pay around £300 for a new one, but they can be found quite cheaply second hand.

It has to be said that home made smokers will probably never be as satisfactory as bought ones in terms of their fixtures and fittings. Perhaps this is just a reflection of my own DIY skills, but I have found the trays used in professionally made smokers to be ideal for the job and, whereas the racks I have botched up to hang fish from are fine, I have had difficulty in keeping cheese.

The common smoker sold in UK shops looks a little like an antique fridge, and does its job very well. There are others that look like long tubes of stainless steel where the smoke is generated in the bottom, and some that look a little like 'Stephenson's Rocket,' with posh wheels to boot.

However effective these machines are in producing a product, it has to be said there is always an element of cooking. The smoke does not always arrive cool, and it is in this respect that the homemade comes into its own. I have seen converted caravans, garden sheds, portaloos and even tents used as a smoker where the smoke is separated from the food by around 5 to 10 metres of hose to cool it.

Perhaps the best smoker I have seen consisted of a firebox on an old wood burning stove, a ten metre length of ducting to a galvanised burning bin (the kind used in the garden for burning old rubbish) into which the smoke was delivered via the flue in the bin lid. The fire was purchased second hand for £20 and the ducting and burning bin cost about the same. (On the Internet I did see a smoke generator attached to a cardboard box via some tumble dryer ducting, all held together with duct tape. The box only lasted a single session, but it did work. After the smoking session was over the cardboard box was simply soaked in water and put on the compost heap.)

The resulting food is not cooked. With many smoking machines the food starts to cook, albeit very slowly, which to my mind is no bad thing, but you do need to ensure that the food has been heated to a temperature high enough to kill any germs there may be inside, and that the food has been correctly cured in the first place. Just imagine a chicken kept at 30°C for six hours; the space betwixt muscle and bone will be well and truly sodden with bacteria.

A good meat thermometer is a great buy and a great tool for feeling secure about the safety of your food. If you know for certain that the centre of your meat has been heated to 75°C for fifteen minutes you can say for certain that it is safe. At the same time add a good pair of insulating gloves and a whole bag of surgical gloves to your shopping list, especially if you have sensitive skin.

Wood for smoking

You can buy briquettes that are specially designed for various smokers. Ash, hickory, oak, birch, pine, tea and sandalwood will all give specific flavours to the food; these are detailed as appropriate in the recipe pages. You can, of course, use wood shavings but do be aware that you will need quite a few shovels full if you are going to smoke a batch of herrings for six hours.

In a home made, fire based smoker a small fire is started, preferably with charcoal, and is then smothered with shavings or dust. The fire initially seems to go out, but shortly thereafter it will begin to smoulder and smoke. This smouldering and smoking must be maintained for up to eight hours and the temperature of the smoke tested to make sure it is still cool. You will have to experiment with quantities and times to find a product you really like.

Smoking can be an expensive business in that you will face a significant outlay if you choose to buy the equipment. Alternatively, if you decide to build your own home made set up you will need to invest a lot of your own time into the project. Do take into consideration the fact that the food will still need to be cooked once it has been cured and smoked, except perhaps in the case of certain sausages (and even these I would prefer to cook). This simple fact might make the hot smoking option the easier of the two methods.

Wood types and their flavours vary considerably, as does the way the wood is prepared. A new, green wood will produce a different smoke to a dried, seasoned wood. New wood has a lot of moisture and contains various chemicals that can add an acrid flavour. This is particularly true of rose.

Alder

This is used almost exclusively with fish, particularly salmon, but I have also used it to smoke burgers with great success.

Apple

This is sweet, and at its sweetest when freshly cut. It is also relatively mild. Apple also does not give an acrid flavour when new.

Cherry

This is a fruity, resinous wood when fresh, with a sweet flavour.

Hickory

This is an excellent flavour for stronger meats and sausages. It is quite pungent.

Maple

People usually describe this is a sweet wood for smoking, similar to maple syrup.

Oak

This is a brilliant, strong flavour for bacon.

Rose

A very fragrant and strong flavour, rose is good to mix with other woods for added body.

Hot smoking

In this system the chamber gets hot and cooks the food whilst imparting a smoked flavour. In many ways this method suits modern living because we can cure and freeze the food and then do the smoking and cooking in a single process. Kippers, for example, are superb done in this manner. The prospect of this alone means that fishing for herring, then salting a bucket full and bringing them home to stock the freezer gives you a really good feeling of well-being, as though you have stocked up a secure supply of food from the wild.

The hot smoker in its simplest form is basically a lidded steel box with a tray inside. It is not much more than a barbecue really. In fact they can be used on an ordinary barbecue. They can even be used indoors as they do not emit huge quantities of smoke.

You simply sprinkle your wood shavings on the base of the tin and put your food on the grill of the barbeque or the hob. It is usually best if the food is put on a tray or some foil to catch the drips of oil and fat that might actually set the shavings alight or to catch juices that could put out the lightly smouldering wood.

The smoker can become very hot and it is remarkable how well the lid keeps most of the smoke inside the space. Cooking times can vary from 10 minutes for a lightly smoked piece of fish to 20 minutes for a chicken breast.

The low salt bacon cure recipe mentioned in Chapter 3 is wonderful cooked in this way. Do remember, though, that this is for flavour only and does not preserve the food in any way, although it does cook and smoke it at the same time. To my mind it is infinitely better than adding powdered smoke to food as it's the real thing.

You cannot really smoke cheese by this method unless you like to eat something a little like smoked Welsh rarebit. That said, it is my own view that smoking is a terrible thing to do to a good cheese anyway.

Another benefit of this set up is that you can use it as a steamer, or combine steam and smoke. You simply place a shallow dish of water in the bottom and the wood dust next to it. This produces a very mild cooked product, but it can get a little bit messy.

Everything that was said about using cured food does not apply to hot smoked food, except in the case of sausages, which are kept following cooking for some time. You can make cooked sausage which is hot smoked, but it will lose fat, and consequently cure with it, so the sausage can really only be kept for no more than a couple of weeks. Air-dried smoked sausage such as poloni and chorizo is best cold smoked.

However, hot smoked ordinary sausages are fantastic, the hot smoker being a very convenient way of cooking them

Smoking bacon

Starting with a cured piece of belly pork (supposing that is the cut you desire, which it should be because it's gorgeous!) you will need to dry it completely. This is not as simple as you might first suppose. Yes, you can pat it dry with paper towels, but this would not quite make it ready for smoking. Instead simply leave it in a very well ventilated room until the proteins near the surface begin to leave a slight coating.

When smoking whole pieces of meat, hooks are useful, and you can get plastic ones as well as metal ones. Similarly, you can use meat hangers, which are a kind of coat hanger with a sprung or tensioned clasp with which you grip the meat for smoking. If you have made your own smoker from a fridge you can actually lay your meat on the racks, but these will get messy after a while. You could even lay your meat on a plate, but you would have to turn it over at some point so that it was evenly smoked.

A purpose built smoker should have some built in, if rudimentary, temperature control. If you have made your own you will have to learn the techniques for controlling your fire to keep it smouldering. A good thermometer, preferably a simple and easy to clean glass one, is also a useful tool. Do remember that if you are smoking outside in the summer a box may naturally heat up to over 30°C without any smoke, so you would do well to restrict your smoking to cold days if this is the case.

Whole pieces of meat need to be smoked for at least eight hours. Some people smoke for days on end, but you will have to make your own mind up depending on the conditions, the fat content of the food and the type of wood.

Storage

Well salted and smoked bacon should last for three months or more. If you slice the bacon it will start to deteriorate rapidly, so sliced smoked bacon should be tightly wrapped in cling film. Remove the rind before cooking if you must. Personally, I love the way it becomes hard and crispy when fried.

Smoking bacon slices

This can sometimes be a hit and miss process, and it simply isn't worth getting out the cold smoker for a few slices of bacon. It can be done, however. They need to be dried and smoked very lightly for about an hour. Avoid resinous wood. I have made a decent product using tea leaves. (There's an old joke about Yorkshire men there somewhere, but being from Lancashire I think it is in poor taste!)

Hot smoking bacon is only done with slices because there is not much room in the machine for a whole piece of meat. It takes around fifteen minutes to create a well-smoked, well-cooked product. I have frequently smoked the sliced bacon and then finished it off in the frying pan because I tend to prefer it crispy.

Smoked ham

Cold smoked hams have an interesting flavour. I prefer them oak smoked, and it will take around eight hours to complete the job. They should be smoked after their hanging period, having been washed and dried. (Washing is done mostly to remove the salt that may have collected on the surface and might not always be necessary.)

The ham can be hung in cool smoke for at least eight hours. If desired it can be done for days; some recipes actually smoke the hams for three weeks! It is best starting short and finishing long; smoke a ham for six to eight hours and see how you like it, then increase the time until you reach your ideal end product.

Alternative recipes call for the ham to be glazed in honey before smoking. This allows the smoke to adhere to the honey to create a crust, but it tends not to penetrate the ham so much. Other recipes do the same with a mixture of honey and mustard.

A smoked ham is best hung again for a few days for the delicate chemistry to work its way into the meat and, once sliced, should be used fairly quickly.

Smoking hams certainly finds the hairs on the joint, which can stand out like some alien creature but are consequently very easily snipped off with a pair of scissors.

Hot smoked chicken

When I was a child, chicken was considered an expensive meal. The production of chicken, then all free range, had not kept pace with the demands of the chicken eating population and so we invented Orwellian factories to rear them by the billion.

Hot smoked is an excellent way of serving chicken, particularly if you use something mild like apple. The meat can become a little discoloured and may even become slightly gelatinous in nature. To offset this I often use smoked chicken pieces in a casserole, deep fry them or toast them under the grill.

Smoked Salmon

People eat smoked salmon raw, so a thorough curing before smoking is absolutely essential. Use curing salt and inject it into the thickest part of the flesh as well as soaking it in cure for 24 hours.

The fish should already be filleted and cleaned, preferably frozen to disrupt any fleas or sea lice (these can be a problem with some farmed salmon) which might occasionally be present. You might need to 'tweezer' out some of the bones. The fish should be kept cold at all times and smoked at a temperature no hotter that 25°C. Use any hardwood although oak is the traditional choice and smoke it for around 12 hours. The fish looks like smoked salmon, if you will pardon the description. It will look glazed.

You can then rinse the fish although this is not obligatory. Store it in a sealed bag in the fridge or freezer. As with any raw food, do serve it sparingly and sliced very thinly until the skin is met.

Kippered Salmon

This is another term for hot smoked salmon. It still needs to be cured as above, but is cut into serving sized portions and then hot smoked. The resulting kippers can be served hot or sealed in a bag once cool and kept for a week.

Kippers

The word kipper, or the Dutch word 'kuppen,' referred at first to spawning salmon. It actually means 'spawn' and described the salmon rushing up river to mate. Today, of course, kippers are cured smoked herring with their heads and guts removed and then split into two. Kipper fillets are the halved versions.

They are cured in brine for a few hours, dried and then smoked, usually in something like hickory. Herring caught on a line should be killed, gutted as soon as possible afterwards and put straight into salt. They should be cured for around six hours after which they should be washed, dried and lightly smoked. Traditionally, herring are salted in barrels, the pickle being formed by the liquid that exudes from the fish under the salt. Cold smoked herring can take days, even weeks, but at home it is probably best to continue for between six and eight hours.

Once smoked the product needs to be consumed fairly quickly, if only due to the fact that the smell can invade almost anything. That said, it is a very homely smell. You can pack them in vacuum bags if available and refrigerate them where they will last for several weeks, assuming you have the willpower and self-discipline.

Hot smoked kippers are actually an approximation of the kipper. They can be smoked and served in a single sitting which is, in my opinion, the most convenient way of cooking them.

Chapter Seven
Smoking cheese

The subject of smoking cheese has kept me sleepless for many a night, sad man that I am! Cheese is one of those materials which, if you leave it outside for even the shortest of times, will acquire a hard crust, and the merest hint of heat will then melt it, separating the fat from the protein.

At one time I adored Austrian Smoked Cheese, which was a simply processed cheese, extruded into a sausage shape, then smoked. In truth was both false flavoured and processed.

Smoking cheeses requires a cool smoke, and to achieve this you will need a cold smoker. We have already detailed how you can make these, but what about those of you who do not have room for such equipment?

Cold smoking

The best way to begin cold smoking a cheese is to leave it outside for a few hours to develop a bit of a crust. It simply dries the cheese a little which will enable the smoke to adhere more easily.

I have found it best to smoke with apple which produces a mild flavour, but you must make sure that the temperature is cool by frequently checking the thermometer. At no time should the temperature rise above 25°C. If you are doing this in the summer the ambient temperature on a hot day alone could well be sufficient to begin cooking the cheese.

You will have to experiment with smoking times. I am afraid I cannot really give you guides because it will always be such a personal thing. Personally I like my own cheese so much that I wouldn't wish to change its flavour in any way, but when I have attempted to do so I have had good results after just four hours.

Maturing the cheese after smoking is an interesting process. The bacteria inside continue to mature, save for an ever-decreasing ring on the outside. This can produce an interesting range of flavours in the same cheese. It can also look very impressive on the cheese board.

Some like it hot

Hot smoking cheese will usually be pretty disastrous. The fat will separate and then you will have a gooey mess. Processed cheese, or American Cheese, is made in factories from a special blend of off-cuts and what I like to call 'sweepings up,' all boiled together and sometimes smoked. The trick is to keep the protein and fat emulsified. This is achieved by adding emulsifying agents such as epsom salts and a lot of stirring.

Processed cheese sets and can be made at home but it is a messy process. Begin by breaking up your cheese into small pieces and put it on a low heat with a small amount of water. A teaspoon of epsom salts is added and you can then start to stir. This is a vigorous process that hopefully will result in a homogenized mass. This can then be placed into a hot smoker and removed every couple of minutes for a stir. The total smoking time should not be more than 30 minutes.

Alternatively you can add some cream, ideally the same weight as the cheese, and stir it every couple of minutes. You will end up with a smoked fondue that will not set.

A more creative use of the hot smoking machine is to achieve the effect of smoked cheese in certain dishes.

Smoked gratin

There are a number of dishes that are topped with cheese melted under the grill. If you put the mixture into a shallow dish and then into the smoker with grated cheese of any type on the top, the cheese portion of the dish will be smoked and will melt at the same time, thus completing your course as though you had used smoked cheese in the first place.

Smoked rarebit

Create your rarebit sauce in the normal way and toast your bread. Before you combine the two make a boat for the bread using foil so that it fits snugly all around but allowing space for the topping.

Add the topping and a little extra grated cheese and finish it off in the smoker. The foil protects the bread but lightly smokes the top so that the effect is as if you had used smoked cheese.

Smoked Pizza

This is a bit messy, but great fun. Make your own pizza in the normal way. I suppose, if you must, you can buy one and still follow the recipe.

When you check the pizza in the oven, say after five minutes, remove and cut it into segments and return half of them to the oven, but sprinkle a little extra cheese on the others prior to smoking. You could protect the base with foil if you prefer not to have smoked bread.

Then present them in an alternate smoked / non-smoked pattern after cooking.

Smoked Pasta

One of our favourite dishes is bacon pasta. It is so easy to make, being little more than fried bacon pieces, cream, milk and sometimes a little onion or garlic with a huge handful of cheese, all melted in. The pasta is boiled and combined. It is a meal that takes no more than fifteen minutes to complete.

This can be finished in the oven to give a crispy top, or sprinkled with more cheese and placed in individual dishes to be hot smoked.

You can replace the bacon with prawns or shrimp, in fact with almost anything you like, and of course the bacon can be smoked too!

Chapter Eight
Your First Smoke

This chapter will guide you through making a boiled ham and using a hot smoker for the first time. I am hoping that you are a complete newcomer to making your own food if you have now become sufficiently inspired to have a bash.

The first thing you will realise is that your kitchen is really designed more for opening tins and warming their contents than for actually making food. I found I didn't have enough space, a sink full of utensils that needed washing before I could pour my boiling liquor away, nowhere to cool things properly and certainly no place to store a ham soaking in brine.

Getting the meat for the ham

Although I have since used my own pig meat, my very earliest attempts were made with pieces of pork shoulder I had bought. It is now something I do often just because it is easy and cheap. I must say that a boiled ham is really best made from a leg, but my first ham was made using a piece of shoulder, and it just happens to illustrate very well the difference between what you might expect and what you actually do get in practice.

The shoulder is the bit you usually scratch on the pig and it is curious to think that many people believe the joint comes off the animal in a cylindrical shape. Of course we all know it is flat! To illustrate the vast range of misconceptions harboured out there I cite my mother who has lived for seventy years but has only just realised that boiled ham is pork!

The skin itself does not absorb very much salt so it needs to be cut off. You may well remember old-fashioned boiled ham; it always had some fat on it, so leave some. You should now have before you a piece of flat meat that you can start to salt.

Making the brine

In theory this is a simple process, but most people do not have a container big enough to contain the meat and the salt. My first time, and many a time since, the job was done in one of those big plastic storage boxes with a lid. You don't have to keep it in the kitchen.

The ever reliable egg test is fine for making ham but don't make the mistake of pouring the water into a container so wide that the egg cannot float in it because the liquid is too shallow. Add the salt for the cure, giving it a good stir, and then, once you have the egg floating, you can add the sugar. The simplest cure is made of two parts salt to one part sugar.

Dunking the meat

Dissolve everything before you add the meat, which will float in the cure. Weigh it down with a plate. Turn the meat over every day and have a good smell of it. You will notice that where the plate touches the meat the blood will show a little, but once you turn it over and re-soak it the stain goes away.

How long should I cure? How long do you wish to keep it? In our house boiled ham doesn't last that long, so I soak it for four days because it only needs to keep for a week if we're lucky. You, on the other hand, might not have a tribe of hungry rugby players to feed and so it might need more salting, say for around a week.

Watch out for the scum that may appear on the curing liquid and scoop it off. If the meat is really thick then consider injecting the very centre with brine too. Brine pumps are easy to use as you cannot overdo it because any excess simply escapes from the meat.

In my early days I would spend ages looking at the meat and wondering if it was thick enough to inject in the knowledge that if I didn't inject I would spend the remaining time worrying about not having done so! It is just the unknown at work on the imagination. If your meat is two to three inches thick, don't worry but if you are going to make a ham out of a huge pig's leg then go for a pump or four of brine injected right into the meat.

The meat will fall apart a little in the brine. A cheap cut from the supermarket is never a work of art and there are always going to be bits of muscle pointing in all sorts of directions so your cured meat might end up looking a little like road kill. The meat will have lost water, even though it has been floating about in liquid for a week, and will consequently look a strange colour and somewhat ragged.

The thing to realize is that, unless you have used curing salt, and I seldom do for something we eat all the time, there will be a change in colour. Uncooked, the meat will look darkish with a slightly greyish hue.

Boiling

I prefer to boil things well, having been educated at the belt and braces school but you can overdo it. I certainly did the first time. I boiled the meat for an hour and a half and, after forty-five minutes,

I changed the water to reduce the salt. This was a good course of action as the meat had just the right saltiness, but in every other respect I cannot describe it as my finest ham moment.

First of all I rolled and tied the meat into a joint, like it was when I had first bought it. But there were bits sticking out and I wasn't able to force them in because the meat was nothing like the consistency it had been. When I boiled it my inept attempt to tie the joint in position was revealed as the meat opened itself up, not so far as to be completely flat, but certainly not like a traditional boiled ham you might buy in the shops. Of course, this wouldn't have happened if I had used a piece of leg.

What I had tasted as boiled ham should but it looked like roast pork. Worst of all it was very dry. The boiling had made the meat fall apart a little and a course grained meat dries out very quickly. It is here that a thermometer comes into its own. It is not, perhaps, considered very manly to have to use a thermometer, but if you can boil the ham for the appropriate time so the centre of the meat reaches 75°C for fifteen minutes, then this is all you need.

The problem was that in my head I had the idea of a perfect sandwich with a nicely shaped and cut slice of pinkish meat. What I actually got looked so unlike the product that I wondered why I had bothered. Then I made a sandwich and gave it to the world's foremost critic of ham sandwiches, my son. The look on his face as he magically made the plate of sandwiches (or butties, as we call them) disappear, confirmed that I was actually on to a winner.

Since then I have made champion boiled hams and how I wish there could be competitions for pork pies and boiled and roast hams as there were in Victorian times. We need these skills more than ever today because if all we do is buy food from the supermarket they will be lost forever. The evidence suggests that pig meat has been cured in this country for many thousands of years whereas the supermarkets have only been in existence for a few decades.

Smoking

It is more probable that most of us will start hot smoking before cold and the numbers of us who actually cold smoke will be few in comparison. Our smoker is an excellent American lidded pan with a close fitting top and a few packets of wood shavings. It is not pan shaped, but is actually more like a large tray. Inside there is a grill on which the food is placed and you simply put the shavings in the base.

The book that came with the smoker had some questions in it. One said, "What do I do if the smoker gets all blackened?" The answer was a straight forward 'Nothing! That's what is supposed to happen!'

This was the best advice I could have read because it set me free from trying to do it all cleanly. But it did worry me that the kitchen would fill with smoke, and then there was the problem of washing up!

I decided to put the wood dust on a sheet of aluminium foil and placed another loosely on top so that any drips from the food wouldn't set it alight. (Try smoking a pork chop without fat going all over the place and see how you do!)

I set the smoker on the cooker and turned it on high. This was the scary bit. Normally you put pans on the cooker with liquid in them and the liquid moderates the force of the heat. I imagined a ruined cooker, a kitchen full of smoke and a melted and misshapen piece of metal containing the charred remains of my dinner somewhere within.

In truth the process was quite painless. The pan got hot, but not too hot to hold the long handles. The wood smoked but you could only just smell it in the kitchen and the air was not filled with plumes of smoke. In fifteen minutes there were, however, two chicken breasts cooked and smoked to perfection. There was actually much less skill needed than for boiling a ham.

Fish was the same, although I did add an extra piece of foil over the grill in the smoker to hold the fish together. Making kippers from salted herring caught off the coast of Anglesey proved to be great fun. After being caught they had lain gutted and headless in a plastic box of salt until their awaited appointment with the smoker. (I always store them headless because I don't like fish heads on my food; they seem to smile at me all the time).

The fish had remained in the box for around three days and had lost a lot of water and become pale, dried and crystallised in the salt. I decided to soak them in water for a day before using the hot smoker.

In order to test the saltiness I put a small piece in the microwave and 'zapped' it for a minute then continued to soak it until it was fine. In all this took about eight hours and something like three changes of water for around five fish.

Of course there is nothing to stop you just buying the fish fresh and smoking them right away. Kippers can be smoked in oak for days and days but I have to confess that I have never tried this for myself. Oak smoked herring, on the other hand, is truly fantastic after just thirty minutes in the smoker. It is not quite the same as a kipper, but in its own way it is certainly good enough.

The sole disappointment came from the fact that the colour was different, but I have to say that the bones were much easier to deal with than the veritable nest of needles that had always put me off kippers.

Chapter Nine
Thinking of Selling?

Earlier in this book I stated my belief that the very best food you can get is cooked in your own kitchen. The best advert for this is the army of small farmers and producers who are committed to selling the very best produce. The Farmers Market is the ideal outlet for such enterprises but I well remember the 'egg man' who sold his own eggs, butter, cheese, bacon, lemon cheese and piccalilli on an inner city Manchester market for decades.

He lived just up the road from me in Oldham and had a small farmlet (which I know is not a word but it describes what I mean) supplemented by half a dozen allotments. He drove his food to market in a Reliant three wheeler, just like the Trotters in 'Only Fools and Horses.' Ordinary folk like me could buy the very best food, truly free range and un-interfered with, killed by him in his back shed, both pigs and poultry together. We even used to contribute to the pigs' development by saving our 'swill' and his lad would come and pick it up every Thursday. In exchange for the 'swill' we got a turkey at Christmas.

Those days are long gone but it does show that real food can still be brought to the masses if we have a mind to do so. Today, of course, there are strict laws governing the sale of food to the public. You certainly wouldn't get away with slaughtering your own animals or collecting waste to boil up for pig feed but even given those requirements there are still many quality producers heroically toiling to put food of no less a quality on our plates. If this book in any way serves to inspire you to become the next one then I can feel truly proud of that achievement.

Economics

As I write this, I am making a boiled ham. Home reared, the meat would have cost me around £2.50; it is a piece of leg, skinned with a nice ring of shallow fat. Most of the fat has been removed and it is now sitting in a simple cure of plain salt and dark demerara sugar. After a week it will be removed and boiled. In total this kilo of boiled ham will cost me £3.00 at the absolute maximum yet in my local supermarket the same product, (well not exactly the same because the supermarket ones have a few preservatives thrown in and the pigs wouldn't have had such a privileged life) costs £10.00 a kilo and was no doubt made by a machine. If I was to smear the joint with honey and push cloves into the fat before roasting it, this gorgeous ham would easily sell for £15.00 a kilo.

Regulations

In recent years the rules for food production and sale have been unified across Europe and in the UK there is a very strict regime which everyone must follow, regardless of the size of the company. One-man bands have to go through the same set of hoops as the multi-national conglomerates.

As a very first step you have to register your intention to produce food for the public with your Local Area Food Inspector. The Town

Hall will have the appropriate contact details. This must be done no later than a month before you plan to start producing in order to give the Food Inspector a chance to visit you, talk you through what he is looking for and to assess your facilities.

Way before this you should have made contact with them to explain your plans. They will send you all the relevant booklets that you need to plan your business. Do remember that if you register too soon you might not be ready for the Inspector to realistically assess your premises.

You have to register if you only produce one or two products a week or if you produce hundreds of tons.

You will need a documented food safety system (HACCP). The paperwork for this is not something you simply write, but must be something you can prove you actually do to reduce the risk to the health and safety of your prospective customers.

You will need to prove that your food is safe from contamination when produced, stored, transported and sold.

You will need a documented process by which you prove and adhere to cleanliness and contamination control. How will you separate the inputs into your business, both meat and raw materials, and make them fit for consumption? How will you prove the age and suitability of the raw materials and how will you know if something is wrong?

You will need to prove that you can recognise when something has gone wrong at each stage of the process and how you will put things right.

The basic rules might be different from locality to locality because they are designed to reflect the region for which the food is produced, but the same high standards are fundamental to all areas.

The best advice, if you are thinking of making and selling farmhouse food, is to make contact with your food inspector at your own Local Authority, and they will talk you through the processes and help you to plan your business.

Labelling

Here you are on to a winner as a small producer. Your intention will probably be the production of as natural a product as is possible rather than seeking to provide a product designed to sit for ages on a shelf. Celebrate this fact! Your products will not have the shelf life of something in the supermarket but you can truly describe it as completely fresh which it will be.

If you are selling food to the public you have to prove and show exactly what is in your product. The words 'Farmhouse Low Salt Bacon' are fine so long as you show how much salt per 100g there is in the product. Now, with our recipe for low salt bacon, you can say exactly how much there is, and make a big fuss about it on the packaging, on your notice board or banners, or simply as you shout it from the stall.

Supermarkets and larger food manufacturers have good reasons to keep the public guessing about what is in their food but you can make a point of telling your customers what is in yours!

Value added

If you sell best quality beef or pork that is one thing, but there is an extra mark up in providing the best quality processed food. A further step is to sell your food ready to eat. Country food served at country events means that you can sell your produce at a premium price because not only are you offering food of the highest quality but you are also providing a service to match.

Although this book is in no way intended as a business plan for a catering concern it does seem to me that there are lots of people willing enough to try to make money to keep them on their smallholdings. With good fittings, displays and produce there is every reason to believe that with an appropriate willingness to work at it they can succeed in doing so.

Gourmet

There are a number of possibilities for selling your produce if you link yourselves with the growing number of sausage/curing shops who sell smoking machines, sausage stuffers, cures and mixes. They are growing all over the country and they regularly put on events in pubs and restaurants. There is surely plenty of scope for others to join in with these possibilities.

Chapter Ten
Making your own Smoker

Smoking has been around for thousands of years, and so have designs for smokers and smoking houses. Gone, though, are the times when every fishing community had its own village smoker, which was often nothing more elaborate than a vented shed or tower a little like a Kentish Oast house used for drying hops.

The fire on the floor was always sufficiently far away from the food so that the smoke had cooled by the time it reached its target and consequently smoke houses could be reasonably large structures or might have had smoke vented in from a separate facility.

Modifying a Garden Shed

Those of you with a commercial bent will recognise the need for a large volume of smoke to finish a lot of produce. A newly modified garden shed is an ideal starting point. Some important considerations

must, however, be borne in mind. Make the walls flat so that resin, dust or indeed any germs do not collect on ledges. A good idea is to line the interior of the shed to make them flat. They can then be cleaned as necessary. Similarly, make the roof space fall proof. You do not want anything falling onto the food. For this reason it must also be animal proof too.

A lining of sheet steel would be ideal, but suitably proofed ply will probably do just as well. Discuss through your plans with your local food inspector; you will generally find them very helpful and if you have incorporated their suggestions they will certainly see you as being of little risk to the public health!

Smoke

Ideally the smoke source should be some distance away from the shed. A simple smoke generator will probably not be big enough to fill an average shed so an alternative will be needed. A modified metal box such as an old fashioned bread bin will generate smoke. Cut a hole in the side and use an appropriately fashioned metal tube to duct the smoke.

Around two feet of this will render the smoke cool enough not to damage flexible hosing such as that used in a clothes dryer which you can attach to your metal tube to deliver the smoke over the remainder of its route to its final destination and the food to be smoked. The fire can be made in the bottom of the box and then smothered with sawdust. Another alternative would be to place it on a barbeque with the sawdust inside to smoke and smoulder away.

Above all you need to ensure your smoke generation does not pose any kind of fire risk, and if you have employees they too will need to be protected and have a well-rehearsed and documented contingency should the need arise.

The easiest way of ducting into the shed is by drilling a hole in the wall. A better solution, however, is to modify a cat flap which can then be set into place and easily made air tight.

If at all possible you should include a vent which can be opened or closed in the top of the shed. A sliding metallic window vent would be adequate for this purpose.

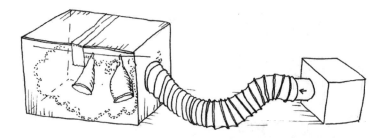

Bradley produces a stand alone smoker which delivers reasonably cool smoke to their own smoking cabinets. They work by automatically dropping a briquette of wood onto a hot plate which causes them to smoke. This is really designed to feed the Bradley cabinet, but can also be fixed very easily to an old fridge. All you have to do is use a circle cutter on a hand drill to cut a hole at the right height. The smoker can then be inserted into the fridge.

If you place a cowl onto the smoke generator, this can then be ducted anywhere to allow all kinds of simple smoking. The simplest I have seen is a cardboard box all taped up with a hole cut out and the ducting taped securely to it. This box works just fine and can be composted or disposed of after use.

Dustbin smokers

Removing the floor of a new galvanised metal dustbin is no mean feat but putting enough holes in it to allow the smoke access is somewhat easier. A fire pit smoker can be made very easily. Simply sink a metal box (like the bread bin above) into the earth and start a fire in it, covering with sawdust to make it smoke.

Place the laden dustbin (laden with your food, that is) over the smoking fire and leave the lid ajar for ventilation. You have to watch this because if the fire is too hot the food will cook. With practise you can gauge the size of fire needed to produce just enough smoke.

An extension of this method is to punch only one hole in the dustbin and deliver the smoke using a drainpipe as in the illustration below.

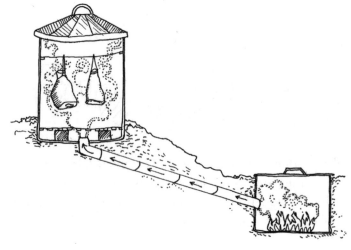

Breeze Blocks

The fascinating thing about breeze blocks is that they are hollow, and as such they can be used to duct, even become a miniature smoke chamber. You can come up with an infinite number of designs although your time may be better spent devising just a couple and then using them to start smoking. Laying the blocks flat along the ground from a fire box will simply deliver smoke along the interior and a holed plate can be used to allow the smoke to be transferred to the vertical. This could be a perforated drum, a structure made from more blocks or even the interior of the blocks themselves. You will not even need to cement the vertical blocks in place although it would be wise to make sure that they form a stable structure and are unlikely to be knocked over by either wind, pets or children!. The beauty of this arrangement is that you can dismantle everything when you have finished.

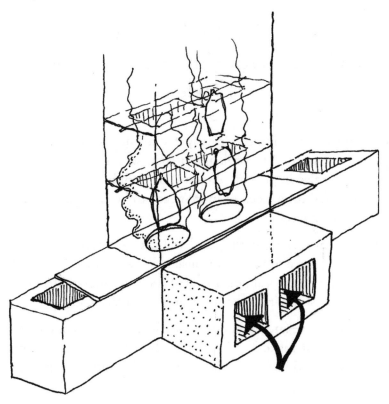

Chapter Eleven
Recipes for Brines, Cures & Pickles

The recipes will indicate clearly if it is imperative to use curing salt as opposed to ordinary kitchen salt. The times required for curing are also important. As a rule of thumb, anything that isn't brined or salted for a week or more needs to be eaten fairly quickly, usually within a week.

Drying is a process of curing, and will take a number of months. Keep to the rules and you will realise how easy a process it is. The big problem is that it is almost too easy and can generate the kind of eagerness that sometimes tends towards complacency.

These recipes have an element of choice within them. They are strict in that you must make a safe product, but they should eventually come to be considered as a guide. Get a pencil out and experiment;

write all over this book and make your amendments. For some the recipes may be too salty and for others they will not be salty enough. As long as you can guarantee a safe product just suit yourself.

Glazes and flavourings need to be thought through before using them. What is the point of making a wholesome home made product and then smearing it with marmalade or jam that is full of preservatives? The very best produce from your garden should be fine, but don't go using pesticide sprays on them. Yes, I know I am probably teaching you to suck eggs.

The recipe for ultra low salt bacon is yours with which to make a million pounds. The only payment I ask is a bacon sandwich.

Measurements

Everything is measured in grams or kilos. There are a number of American recipes on the internet and they have an unusual weights system that is neither metric nor imperial. Their official imperial weights are slightly larger than our old ones, but not so much as to make a great difference.

Do double check the suitability of your brine by doing the egg test, regardless of the recipe and before the other ingredients are added but always remember that it is the salt that cures.

Imperial or US	Metric
1 lb	0.45 Kg (454 g)
1 oz	28 g
1 pint	0.47 l or 470 ml
1cup	240 ml
1 tablespoon	15 ml
1 teaspoon of salt (level)	5 g
1 teaspoon of pepper	2.5 g
1 dash	0.5 g

Bought cures

There are many companies who sell bought cures with everything you need to make a ham, bacon or almost anything else for that matter. They sometimes call for the product to be cured in a separate process, but at other times the whole mix is complete. Just make sure you follow the instructions carefully.

A bought spiced mix can be perfect for creating the ideal boiled ham or air-dried ham too. You can create fantastic dry cured bacon and even get cures with built-in smokiness. Usually the cure is added at 3% - 5% of the weight of the meat. You can also buy organic cures which often use ground sea salt, organic sugars and other ingredients.

Our recipes are for 'make it yourself' cures so that you can build up from scratch. We do not look at mixing salt with saltpetre so be sure to buy it premixed for reasons we have already explored. Enough cure to make around 25kg of bacon costs less than £10.00 at current prices, a huge saving on shop prices for dry cured products. In one family meal you should recover your costs.

Brines for curing and pickling

These mixes will be used in recipes later in the book. You can also use them to experiment, so long as you stick to the rules of cleanliness, the ratios of brine to meat and the time required for curing.

The basic brine mixes allow you to dip your toe in and make something that doesn't cost a lot of money but which may spur you on to greater things.

Basic brine with saltpetre

This makes a gallon of brine, which will easily cure 10kg of meat. However, you can double and triple these numbers easily to make any amount of liquid.

Ingredients for basic brine

1kg of curing salt
300g of brown sugar
5g (1 level tsp) of red pepper
4.5 litres of water

Method

Heat the water in a pan until it is hand hot. It doesn't actually matter if it boils. Add the salt and allow it to cool, stirring to help dissolve it.

When cool, check the concentration using the egg test.

Add all the other ingredients and stir until they are dissolved. Keep it in a sealed container if it is not in use.

The red pepper can be augmented, replaced or removed completely. Alternatives I have used include garlic, mint, sage, onion, aniseed, cloves and celery.

This brine will cure a ham in one month, making sure that the brine is used at a rate of 4.5 litres (1 gallon) to 10kg of meat. It will cure bacon in just two weeks at the same ratio.

§

Basic brine without saltpetre

This makes a gallon of brine, which will easily cure 10kg of meat.

You can add any additional flavouring. The method for making it is as for basic brine with saltpetre.

Ingredients

1kg of plain salt
500g of demerara sugar
5g (1 level tsp) of red pepper
4.5 litres of water

§

Beer brine without saltpetre

This makes a gallon of brine, which will again easily cure 10kg of meat. It has a distinctive flavour and works well for bacon and hams. Use this to give a good colour to pork in lieu of saltpetre.

You can make very sweet and rich hams with this by dressing the meat with honey once it is cured.

Ingredients

1kg of plain salt
300g demerara sugar
3.5 litres of water
1 litre of mild or dark beer

§

Corning cure (wet)

You might need to double this quantity to make more than 5 kilos.
You can add flavours beyond the above such as onion, garlic etc.

Ingredients

750g of curing salt
250g of sugar
25g of black pepper
25g of ground cloves
6 bay leaves
25g of mixed pickling spice
This will be sufficient for 4.5 litres of water.

§

Corning cure (dry)

Ingredients

500g of salt
75g of sugar
1tbsp of cracked pepper corns
1tsp of paprika
1tsp of finely chopped sage
1tsp of crushed bay leaf
2 tsp of allspice
This is the cure for rub in type corned beef recipes.

§

Wiltshire cure

This makes a gallon of brine which will easily cure 10kg of meat.

Ingredients

650g of curing salt
454g of molasses
50g of crushed and chopped coriander
50g of juniper berries (if you can get them)

Wiltshire cure is a very soft mix that tastes sweet and is ideal for bacon. The hams are soaked for three days and then hung and dried.

There are a number of speciality mixes from various professional producers which go under the general title 'Wiltshire.' I cannot guarantee that the above is completely accurate because the recipe is supposed to be a secret, and no one will let me in on it!

Honey brine with saltpetre

This makes a gallon of brine which should easily cure 10kg of meat. It has a distinctive flavour and works well for bacon, particularly with belly.

Ingredients

1kg of curing salt
454g (one whole pot) of local honey
4 litres of water
0.5 litres of rosewater

Do not boil the water when adding the honey. It breaks down to give all sorts of strange flavours. Mix it well and during the brining process make sure that the liquid does not separate at any time. Stirring it frequently will ensure this.

Do not keep this brine for long periods. The chemistry of honey is a mysterious affair and unusual flavours can result. It is ideal for hams that will later be roasted with a honey topping.

Ude's cure

This goes back to Ude, someone who, apart from his recipe, has been entirely lost in the mists of medieval history. It makes a gallon of brine, which will easily cure 10kg of meat.

Ingredients
1kg of curing salt
300g of brown sugar
1 litre of vinegar
5.5 litres of water

First dissolve the salt and sugar in the water and then add the vinegar. This cure is great for boiled ham in the above ratios. You can make the cure more interesting by adding a few handfuls of raisins and when the ham is boiled and served, the raisins can be tipped over it.

Rollmop pickle #1

This pickle is really spiced vinegar, the fish having already been salted and soaked before pickling.

Ingredients

2 onions, very finely sliced (you need a really sharp knife)
2 litres of white vinegar
1 clove for each 500ml of vinegar
1 bay leaf for each 500ml of vinegar
250g finely sliced cucumber

There are many ways of using this pickle. The fish are salted on catching and can be soaked in water for an hour to reduce their saltiness. Cook a piece in the microwave to confirm that it is to your taste before using the fish. Another way of soaking would be to do it in vinegar which is more expensive, but this way you are not diluting the vinegar's efficiency later on as you will by using water. This recipe keeps herrings uncooked.

Rollmop pickle #2

Ingredients
500ml of water
4 litres of vinegar
2 onions, peeled and quartered
2 sticks of celery, chopped

This recipe is best used for the cooking recipe for rollmops.

Fish pickle cure

This is for any number of fish recipes

Ingredients
2 litres of water
2.5 litres of white vinegar
500g of curing salt
250g of sugar
2 onions, very finely chopped
1 cucumber, finely sliced

The salt is dissolved in the water which is then heated to close to boiling. The fish are then removed from the salt and plunged directly into it. Allow it to cool naturally in sterile bottles and keep for it for up to 2 months.
The fish will need to soak in a change of water.

Dry cure with saltpetre

This is the simplest dry cure.

500g of curing salt
250g of demerara sugar

Use the best, most expensive sugar you can find! Do not keep it for a long time to avoid moisture problems.

Jerky cure

There are dozens of jerky cures out there. Simply think about your favourite flavours and incorporate them. This is enough for 1kg of finely sliced meat.

Ingredients

50g of plain salt
25g of crushed black pepper
15g of cayenne pepper
25g of cumin powder
4 crushed garlic cloves

Fish dry cure

Ingredients
500g of curing salt
300g of demerara sugar
10 cracked and ground fresh peppercorns
5g (1tsp) of ground allspice
Try this with pike. It is the best way to preserve this noble fish!

Sweet dry cure for fish

Ingredients
250g of plain salt
500g of brown sugar
25g of ground ginger
25g of ground white pepper
3 crushed garlic cloves

This cure makes great hot smoked salmon and is strong enough to keep the fish for a couple of weeks.

Chapter Twelve
Recipes for Rubs & Smoking

Once you have set out on the road to creating brilliant cured food, begin to compare recipes and make decisions about which method you will use. Curing is a strange mix of art and science. The science bit comes primarily in not killing yourself, friends and other family members by making bad meat. The art comes in making a product that suits your tastes.

These recipes are only starting points on what could become a long but satisfying journey. As long as you remember that you need enough salt to kill germs and that if you are going to keep the meat for any period longer than a week or so, you need saltpetre, then you should be fine.

The cures in Chapter 11 can be substituted by bought ones or modified, as long as you maintain the salt content. Do not try to make a low salt cure. Our ultra low salt bacon cure is nothing more than flavouring, an approximation by which people can enjoy bacon with reduced salt. Under no circumstances should you attempt to transfer this principle to any other form of curing.

In my previous book, *The Sausage Book*, we were able to present neat recipe pages with precise directions for you to follow. Curing is an entirely different kettle of (cured) fish. There are more techniques and there is infinitely more waiting and this unfortunately means that you'll just have to read them in the old fashioned way.

ξ

From bacon to hung ham using a bought spice

The first recipe tackled by anyone new to curing will always seem like an epic process not unlike Columbus's journey to the Americas. The chapter upon which you are now embarking should take you through the stages of using a single set of ingredients to making a number of products of increasing complexity.

Cooking is, in effect, the science of understanding how ingredients react under any set of conditions, and curing is no different. Rather than trying to cure a whole pig's leg which could weigh in at as much as fifteen kilos, start instead with a small piece. Get to know what happens in the processes so that by the time you have made bacon, smoked bacon, boiled a ham, roasted a ham, smoked a ham, air-dried a ham no heavier than a kilo, then one of three, five, ten and fifteen kilos you will be a master curer.

The cure itself is simple. Buy the basic mix from a supplier and mix it in the following proportions: 50g of cure mix, 50g of ordinary salt and 50g of brown sugar for every kilo of meat used in the recipe! Your induction into the curing fraternity will therefore be greatly simplified if you restrict your initial experiments to a single kilo of pork leg.

ξ

Rub in for bacon

Rub in the cure all over the meat; 10% on the rind and 90% on the flesh. Then place the meat in a non-metallic container and store it in the fridge at around 4°C for five days, turning the meat over in the pickle each day, the pickle being the juice that has formed from the combining of the meat juices and the salt.

On the fifth day remove the meat and rinse it under the tap. Do not plunge the meat into water as this will start to remove the cure. Then pat it dry with a clean towel and return it to the fridge on a plate covered with a dish where it should remain for a couple of days prior to slicing. After slicing it should be cooked as you would bacon.

ξ
Rub in for boiled ham

Follow the same process as above but first of all cut off any rind. You can leave a little fat if you wish, according to preference. The fat side of the meat should receive 25% of the cure, and the remainder 75% unless you have cut off the fat completely, in which case the cure should be evenly distributed all around.

Turn the meat as before in its own pickle and, on the fifth day, remove and rinse it, returning it to the fridge for a couple of days prior to boiling. Use a thermometer during boiling to ensure that the meat has remained at 75°C for at least fifteen minutes.

To make a roast ham, parboil for the meat for 30 minutes and roast it for another 30. Prior to roasting you can add all sorts of glazes; honey, marmalade, cloves etc.

ξ
Rub in for air-drying a ham

By now you will have become familiar with precisely what a kilo of pork leg does in cure so let's now go for a hanging ham! This method is very similar to that for making a full sized ham, with only a slight modification in times.

Begin by removing the rind and spread your cure mix as in the rub in for boiled ham. This time, after rubbing the cure all over, wrap it in cling film and leave it for two weeks, after which you should unwrap it, repeating the first step once more with fresh cure mix. Finally, as it is only a small piece of meat, leave it for a further week.

Next, remove the cling film, rinse your meat, pat it dry and leave it in the fridge for 3 days after which you should put it into a container out of the fridge for a further couple of days. This step allows the meat to come to room temperature and naturalise easily.

Cover the meat in lard or duck fat (we are now making a confit out of it) and smother it in breadcrumbs or peppercorns, after which you should hang the meat for a month to mature. The hanging can take place in an old fridge, a cool cellar or a dry shed, in fact anywhere you can guarantee that the temperature is cool (best not do this in summer) and that the relative humidity is lower than 65%. You can test this with a hygrometer. You can buy stretch nets to cover hanging hams and this is highly recommended because it keeps flies away from the meat and stops them laying eggs on it. Still cover it with lard or duck fat prior to covering with the net.

Do not hang your ham in the kitchen even though old books may show pictures of hams above a smoking fire. The changes in temperature and humidity, let alone the variations in aromas that can taint the meat, will make the outcome of your curing far less certain.

A full ham with a bone in it will need to mature for six weeks and will also need to have two lots of fifteen to twenty days curing time. I should personally prefer it if you cooked the meat after curing but if you choose not to do so please do give it a good inspection with both your eyes and nose, remembering that it is essentially raw meat!

ξ

Ultra low salt bacon

This is very easy and very effective. You can vary the amount of salt you add. Commercial bacon will have around 50g of salt per kilo and nitrate and anything else they have decided to add. Your product will have more sugar than salt and will not really be bacon in that it doesn't have the same keeping qualities. To all intents and purposes it is, however, the same, especially if you opt for bacon that has half the salt of commercial varieties.

For your meat, ask your butcher to slice 1 kilo of whichever cut you prefer. Spread these on a tray and weigh out the amount of salt you require. A level teaspoon (5g) is not enough to make it taste like bacon. Two level teaspoons (10g) will give it a mild flavour but will certainly smell like bacon when cooking. Three level teaspoons (15g) will be very defiantly bacon, and it will only contain one third of the salt found in its commercial counterpart.

If you chose to use 4 level teaspoons (20g) it would still be a low salt content but will keep for a little longer, for about a week. Remember that as much as 25g is still only half the salt content of commercial bacon.

Rub in even amounts of salt into the cut slices, being careful to sprinkle only onto the meat, not the fat. Then sprinkle a couple of tablespoons of brown sugar over the meat and rub it in. Now cover them and store them in the fridge overnight.

Fry them as for E & B (as P. G. Wodehouse would have said!)

By way of a digression, were you aware that the scum which forms when you cook bacon actually comes from the injected cure that cannot escape from the meat?

ξ

Bacon (wet)

There are dozens of bought cures for you to experiment with, each of them fantastic in their own way. There is nothing quite like the smell of some of these cures half way through the process, save perhaps for the aroma of home brewing. This recipe uses basic brine without saltpetre which should be made as described in chapter 11. Once made, check the cure using the ever reliable egg test.

Ideally your meat for this particular recipe should be either a piece of belly pork, boned leg or pork loin. It should be placed in a non-metallic container and immersed in the brine, the height of the liquid in the container being at least three times the height of the meat to be cured. It should then be weighed down with a plate and should be turned over each day. If you wish you can replace the brine after three days.

The meat can be removed after five days when it should be given a quick rinse under the cold tap. Place it in the fridge on a covered plate for a couple of days before use.

You can test the meat for saltiness by either frying or heating a small amount in the microwave.

ξ

Bacon (dry)

For this recipe use the dry cure with saltpetre as described in Chapter 11. You will need to weigh out 100g of cure per kilo of meat and you should choose a cut from which you personally would like to make bacon, preferably belly, leg or loin. Rub the cure into all sides of the meat but mostly on the muscle side and place it in a non-metallic, lidded container, ideally not that much bigger than the meat itself.

Each day turn the meat in the pickle that is forming in the container. This should be done for five days and on the sixth day remove it, wash it in running water and place it in the fridge for a couple of days prior to slicing. Remember to check for saltiness, soaking it in water to dilute if necessary.

Hot smoked sweet mustard belly

This is adapted from an old favourite which was, in turn, adapted from someone else (and so on it goes).

Buy some cut belly pork and sprinkle it with a mixture of 100g of ordinary salt for every kilo of meat. Place it in a container for three or four days and then rinse off the salt after which you can soak the mustard in a mixture of two tablespoons of honey and a teaspoon (5g) of mustard powder. Then place the belly pork in a plastic bag with the mixture and refrigerate it. Give the pork pieces a good massage every day for two days so that they are all well covered.

Finally remove and hot smoke them until they are cooked, using either hickory or oak shavings.

ξ

Pig cheek bacon

This meat has more pork flavour than any other cut, but is seldom used in our high tech world. It is also very cheap and makes great bacon. If you cannot cope with a pig's head then get your butcher to cut off the cheeks. You can then use almost any dry cure you prefer, although for simplicity try 150g of curing salt and 50g of sugar for each cheek. You will have to remove the bristles, either by shaving or burning. A kitchen blowtorch is ideal for this.

Pile the faces with cure on both sides and wrap them in cling film, massaging and turning them each day for a week. After this the cheeks can be brushed clean and hung for anything up to three months in a cool dry space. It can be eaten raw like ham, but is best fried or used in a creamy pasta dish.

Soft rabbit

Some people do not like the texture of rabbit but this is an excellent food and should be enjoyed by everyone. It is considerably improved by curing it before cooking. To do this use the dry cure described in chapter 11.

First quarter the rabbit and lay it on around half a centimetre of cure and cover it with an equal amount, leaving it overnight. The next day test a piece of meat for saltiness and soak it for ten minutes if necessary. Then rinse the meat and make a stew using no salt.

These pieces could be cured completely and smoked but fresh rabbit has always been in plentiful supply. There is indeed no better way of keeping your meat fresh than allowing it to hop around on the grass.

Corned beef

This recipe expands on a method described briefly in Chapter 4 and works very well with 2kg of brisket, shin or any cut of meat that is cheap. The earlier method dealt with 5kg of meat and consequently the weights for the cure here are adapted to provide adequate for 2kg. This should consist of:

200g of salt
25g of sugar
1 tsp of cracked pepper corns
0.5 tsp of paprika
1 tsp of finely chopped sage
1 tsp of crushed bay leaf
1 tsp of allspice

Rub the cure into the meat and wrap it in cling film, rubbing and turning it inside the cling film every other day for two weeks. If the meat is cut (i.e. in pieces) then do not rub it after it is wrapped. You will simply need to turn it over.

To cook, simmer the meat in water until it is tender. You can change the water during cooking with fresh boiling water if you prefer a milder taste. The meat should be falling off the bone if it has one. It should then be shredded into a sterilised dish, pressing the shredded meat down to exclude as much air as possible. Finally you can confit the meat with one of the following; melted butter, duck fat or lard. Keep it in the fridge for up to three weeks but eat it within a couple of days of the seal being broken.

Jerky or salt smoked beef

Use the jerky cure described in Chapter 11. You will need to slice 1kg of lean beef so that the strips are about 3-5mm thick. This equates to setting No.8 on my own slicer but you will probably have to make an accurate guess initially. It should be a good thick thin slice, nothing too waif-like, if you understand what I mean.

The cure should be rubbed evenly into all the meat on both sides, making sure you have enough for each slice. Rub and turn the meat in the pickle for 3 days, after which you can rinse it under the tap and pat it dry. It should then be placed on a tray in the oven on the lowest possible setting, with the door open. Around four to five hours later the meat will have dried out and, once cooled, can be stored in a container that excludes water.

There are also recipes for jerky using marinades. One of my own personal favourites uses 100ml of Worcestershire sauce, 100ml of soy sauce, 5g of black pepper, 5g of garlic powder and 5g of onion powder. The sliced meat should be left in the marinade for 24 hours and then dried.

If you prefer, you can dry the jerky in a cold smoker. I like to use oak for the purpose. It will take at least 8 hours or you can hot smoke them for 20 minutes, then finish drying them in the oven as described above. When cooked and dried out you can knock nails in them!

Pork pie

Although recognised as a recipe in itself the pie still has its roots as a method of preserving. In my own view it is probably the single best way of doing so! Quite literally, the simplest way there is and, if made correctly, the meat will last for a month. The simple concept of encasing in pastry can actually incorporate three separate methods of preserving; a crust to protect it, a filling confited in jelly and finally, mildly salted meat. Originally the crust was often discarded but today great improvements in the art of making pastry have confined this barbarian practice to ancient history.

For your filling you can use any pork that is fresh but has not been messed with. What do I mean? Well certainly not the roughest cuts; under no circumstances should you use mince, nor meat on offer unless you are going to eat it straight away. Try to use the leanest pork if only because you are going to add a little fat.

For every kilo of meat you should add a further 75g of fat but definitely not skin! A kilo of filling should give you a nice large round pie of approximately 25cm in diameter.

Cut the meat into 2cm cubes and divide it into three piles. Place one pile into the food processor and whiz it round for thirty seconds, adding the second pile for around 30 seconds longer. Then mix this processed meat with the remaining cubes and the fat, adding 10g of salt and 5g of white pepper for every kilo of meat. If you wish you can replace the pepper with a similar amount of mustard or 2g of mace or even combine all the flavours according to taste. Then mix everything well.

For the crust you will need 200g of flour, 200ml of water, 100g of lard and 2g of salt. For the flour I prefer to use strong bread flour. This should be sifted into a bowl together with the salt, making a well in the centre. The lard is then cubed and placed with the water in a saucepan and brought to the boil. The mixture should be poured into the flour and mixed in very quickly using a wooden spoon.

The mixing of the pastry should be completed using your hands and the pastry used straight away to line a greased pie dish approximately 25cm in diameter. Add the filling and press it firmly down, lastly sealing it with the lid, taking time to make the edges neat. A vent should be made in the middle to allow steam to escape.

The pie should cook for 20 – 30 minutes on Gas 5 or at 200°C and should then be turned down to Gas 4 or 175°C for a further hour. Test it with either a thermometer or a knife. If the blade is too hot to touch and nothing sticks to it when removed, then the pie is cooked.

Near the end of the cooking process, heat up sufficient jelly to fill the pie. The filling will shrink considerably, leaving space.

Using a funnel, slowly fill the pie with jelly until it comes out of the hole. Wait a minute for it to settle and then add a little more. Allow the whole thing to cool before taking it out of the pie dish. This will last at least a fortnight if unopened but I'll bet you can't wait that long!

Jellied eel

To make this recipe you will need a fish stock as described in Chapter 5.

For the uninitiated eel buyer I can confirm that an eel bought from the shop comes headless, tailless and gutted. If you catch your own you must do the same as you will need to sprinkle some rosemary, some sage and perhaps a little basil into the cavity. Then roll and tie up the eel using twine and sprinkle a little nutmeg over it.

Bring 500ml of fish stock to the boil and add your eels to cook for 15 minutes. Remove them when tender and untie them. Then add 15g of gelatine to the stock and, when it has dissolved, pour the liquid over the eels in a presentable dish, allowing it to cool and set.

Rollmops

You can use either of the two rollmop pickles described in Chapter 11 according to your own taste or requirements.

Whether you buy your herring frozen or fresh from the fishmongers, you will need to salt them for 24 hours, covering each fish and placing a new one on top of the previous one. Alternatively, you can leave them for 24 hours in the Basic Brine recipe also in Chapter 11.

Next rinse the fish and fillet it. According to convenience you could fillet before salting but in any case rinse them before the next stage.

Roll each fillet (keeping the skin on!) around a gherkin and put it into a jar (Kilner ones are the best) and cover them with pickle. Remember that the more gruesome you can make the jar look the better as this food is too important to give to either children or underlings so the more unpalatable you can make it look, the better.

A dish called zander

The zander is a great imported pike but this dish can also be used for pike. If you have never caught a pike before do watch your fingers, otherwise you might end up eating a fish stuffed with bits of human flesh. Please kill the fish as soon as it is caught. Remember, it is not food until it is dead and until then it deserves a degree of respect and care, and afterwards just care. Also, remember to always satisfy yourself of both the water quality and the suitability of any fish for the plate if you are catching it yourself.

Fillet and gut the fish; you are looking for two fillets. Then lay it down to salt for 24 hours as for rollmops. You can use either of the rollmop pickles. Lay the fillets flat and pickle them for at least a week.

ξ

Smoked freshwater fish

Use the fish pickle cure outlined in Chapter 11.

I can guarantee that if you like eating needles then almost every freshwater fish will be ideal for this recipe. You need only to buy, catch, kill and fillet the fish. Pike, perch and chub are all good for this. Then cure them for a week after which you can remove and wash them.

Test the flesh by cooking a little and if it is too salty, soak it in water and retest it a little later.

The best way of smoking is to hot smoke them for 30 minutes after which they can be eaten hot or cooled and wrapped in cling film and then eaten within a week. Alternatively they can be cold smoked but this should be done for at least 24 hours.

Kippers

Kippers are simply smoked herring and you will need to make a brine as explained in chapter 11 in order to make them. My own preference is for the beer one!

If you have uncleaned kippers, gut and head them and split them along the back, opening them out. I find they sometimes fall apart. Soak them in the cure for about a day and then gently cold smoke them for at least 24 hours in a mixture of oak and any other wood.

An alternative is to hot smoke them. The herring can be laid to salt and washed clean before cooking in the hot smoker using a mixture of oak and tea (packet tea leaves will do nicely). It is a milder alternative and not really like true kippers at all, but just as nice in a different way.

Beware! If you over smoke anything it will begin to resemble a 60-a-day tobacco smoker's lungs!

Potted Shrimp

This is an example of a confit. You need to boil and clean your shrimp as soon as they are caught. They can then be cleaned, which can be a truly fiddly job. After cleaning put them into a very mild salt solution if you have caught them yourself and need to transport them any distance. This should be 25g of salt to every litre of water.

Drain the shrimp and place them in a sterile ramekin, pressing them down. Sprinkle a little mace and nutmeg on the top and a pinch of paprika into 125g of melted butter. Then pour the butter into the ramekin and make sure that all the air bubbles are removed before the butter sets by gently tapping the ramekins on the table. Be sure to form a seal on the top. Your potted shrimp will last around 5 days, but I bet you can't wait that long!

Salt Cod

This is really the basic way to salt all fish.

Choose thick fillets of cod or a whole gutted fish if you prefer. Place about a centimetre of salt in the bottom of a container and lay the cod on top of it. If it is a whole fish then fill the cavity with as much salt as you can get in. Then cover the fish with yet more salt until it disappears. You can layer the fish if you like.

Inspect the fish after three days. You will need to pour off the liquid and replace the salt, ensuring that you cover anything which is exposed. Simply repeat this until it stops pickling or giving off liquid. It can then be brushed clean and stored in a sealed container.

Smoked Bacon

By now you will have at least half a dozen ways of making bacon but if you are sneaking a preview and have just turned to this page then please go back to read chapter 4 and then the beginning of this chapter.

Having cured the joint, wash and then dry it for 2 days by hanging it in the smoking box or chamber. This hanging will allow the surface to change in texture and will dry the meat a little. This way it will take the smoke much more evenly. A smoked bacon joint needs to be cold smoked for at least 10 hours, preferably using apple for a mild smoke or hickory for a more pungent flavour.

Keep your smoked bacon joint in an airtight box on a piece of kitchen foil which you must change regularly. Then simply slice and cook it. – Yum!

Another way of producing the effect of smoked bacon is to create the basic bacon as normal, then to hot smoke it in order to cook it. If you like it crispy, then after 20 minutes of hot smoking, simply finish it in the frying pan.

This is, of course, an ideal way of smoking our ultra low salt bacon.

Wiltshire cure bacon

This is probably the original best bacon or, if not, at least a very good approximation. You will need to make the Wiltshire Ham cure described in chapter 11 at the appropriate rate for your chosen amount of meat. You will need approximately 600ml of cure for every kilo of meat you use. It must be soaked for at least three days, turning it at least twice a day in the cure. Do use gloves because it will stain!

After at least three days remove your meat and pat it dry. If you can hang it then do so for at least three more days. Otherwise, place it on a large plate and dry it in the fridge. This cure works really well with a piece of pork loin.

ξ

Smoked Salmon

You can buy a full salmon for less than £20 these days, or you can catch one yourself for £50, if you're lucky.

Choose a brine without vinegar and cure your salmon for 24 hours. Soak it for an hour afterwards and then leave the fish to dry for 24 hours. You must smoke it gently, with the fish on a tray and with a mild wood for 15 hours, turning the fish several times. Make sure the tray does not get hot. You will see a change in colour in the fish as it smokes and dries further. Eat it within a week, or cook it.

Smoked salmon was never intended as a cured and preserved dish, but one to be eaten by rich folk at parties. Do not keep this food for more than a few days. The ordinary folk, if they were ever able to poach a salmon, either sold it or cooked and ate it quickly.

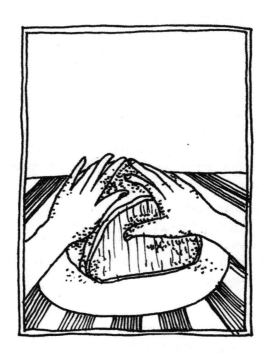

Resources and Useful Contacts

One might have said, some years ago, that everything you need for curing and smoking was at hand in the kitchen. But in those days there would have been no need for a book like this because everyone knew how to make a brine and to make their own bacon or boil a ham.

Sadly, today this is not the case and we find ourselves living in homes with kitchens that are useless for anything other than opening packets and tins, warming their contents or making very expensive posh food.

So you might need to buy a few things. The biggest problem most of you will find, like me, is living in a house without a larder. Different from a pantry, a larder is a large room where food manufacture takes place. In it you can hang hams for drying, store soaking cheeses and hams, pickling fish and what not.

To compensate I personally do all my curing in large sealable plastic boxes. They are easy to clean and can be placed anywhere. I have bacon curing like this in the dining room, though you wouldn't know it as there is no smell or mess.

Most of the ingredients for the cures can be bought from the supermarket. You can obtain non-iodised salt, all the sugars and the various vinegars. However, you will have to buy your actual cure mixes and curing salt with saltpetre from a specialized supplier. You will probably not be able to buy saltpetre directly from the chemist these days, and, as we live in suspicious times, I wouldn't even try to do so.

Ascott Smallholding Supplies.
The Old Creamery, Four Crosses, Llanymynech, Powys,
SY22 6LP. www.ascott.biz. 0845 130 6285
You can buy more or less everything here from smokers to presses and a whole lot more besides.

Crocks and Pots
Challock, Nr. Ashford Kent. TN25 4DG.
www.crocksandpots.com 01233 740529.
This company sells the very best quality pots and pans, knives and other kitchen equipment.

Designasausage
Designasausage, 133 London Road, Macclesfield, Cheshire, SK11 7RL. www.designasausage.com 08452 578884
A friendly shop in Macclesfield, Cheshire run by Janet and Gaynor, a mum and daughter duo. They sell everything from sausage making kits to cures, smokers and presses. They won't sell you anything you don't need.

Weschenfelder
2 -4 North Road, Middlesborough, Cleveland, TS2 1DE.
www.weschenfelder.co.uk 01642 247524
This company have been making sausage skins for over 80 years, but they sell smokers and cures and everything you will need for curing as well as sausage making. You can get a whole lot of friendly advice too!

Bradley Smokers
4 Halwell Business Park, Halwell, Totnes
Devon, TQ9 7LQ
www.bradleysmoker.co.uk. 0845 665 0728
The official website of the best selling smoking equipment. Full of info and links, it also includes a forum with lots of helpful tips from users.

Mundial
Zeva, Unit A, Waterfold Business Park, Bury, BL9 7BR
www.mundial.uk.com 0161 763 6868
They have the best knives anywhere and they will last you a lifetime, even if they do cost a bit.

Scobies Direct
1 Singer Road, East Kilbride, Glasgow, G75 0XS
www.scobiesdirect.com. 0800 783 7331
You will find everything you could possibly want for the butcher and anyone dealing with their own meat here. You can buy netting, casings, packaging and machines. It is well worth a look if you are planning to sell your own produce.

By the Same Author

The Sausage Book
Paperback
192 pages
ISBN 9781904871446

With more recipes than ever, this book makes a wonderful introduction to the world of sausage making. Whether your intention is to make a couple of pounds for the family freezer or expand the range for sale in your shop, The Sausage Book gives step-by-step instructions, as well as an improved recipe section covering over 90 kinds of sausage, from traditional English bangers to international varieties such as salami, chorizo and frankfurters.

Combined with expert advice on linking and making prize winning sausags as well as a first class resource section, The Sausage Book is regarded by many experts as the ultimate sausage resource for all.

"The book is humorous and well written, and a must for all sausage lovers."
The Sizzler

"Tells you everything you could wish to know...the world is, well, your sausage!"
Foods Matter Magazine.

The Good Life Press
PO Box 536
Preston
PR2 9ZY
01772 652693

The Good Life Press Ltd. is a family run business specialising in publishing a wide range of titles for the smallholder, 'goodlifer' and farmer. We also publish **Home Farmer,** the monthly magazine for anyone who wants to grab a slice of the good life - whether they live in the country or the city. Other Titles of interest:

A Guide to Traditional Pig Keeping by Carol Harris
An Introduction to Keeping Cattle by Peter King
An Introduction to Keeping Sheep by J. Upton/D. Soden
Build It! by Joe Jacobs
Build It!.....With Pallets by Joe Jacobs
Building Fences and Gates by Andy Radford
Craft Cider Making by Andrew Lea
First Buy a Field by Rosamund Young
Flowerpot Farming by Jayne Neville
Grow and Cook by Brian Tucker
How to Butcher Livestock and Game by Paul Peacock
Making Country Wines, Ales and Cordials by Brian Cook
Making Jams and Preserves by Diana Sutton
Precycle! by Paul Peacock
Raising Chickens for Eggs and Meat by Mike Woolnough
Showing Sheep by Sue Kendrick
Talking Sheepdogs by Derek Scrimgeour
The Bread and Butter Book by Diana Sutton
The Cheese Making Book by Paul Peacock
The Frugal Life by Piper Terrett
The Medicine Garden by Rachel Corby
The Pocket Guide to Wild Food by Paul Peacock
The Polytunnel Companion by Jayne Neville
The Sausage Book by Paul Peacock
The Secret Life of Cows by Rosamund Young
The Shepherd's Pup (DVD) with Derek Scrimgeour
The Urban Farmer's Handbook by Paul Peacock

www.goodlifepress.co.uk
www.homefarmer.co.uk